FORERUNNERS

Harbingers of Death in Nova Scotia

FORERUNNERS

Harbingers of Death in Nova Scotia

Vernon Oickle

MacIntyre Purcell Publishing Inc.

MacIntyre Purcell Publishing Inc.
232 Fairmont Road
Cloverville, Nova Scotia
B2G 2K9

www.macintyrepurcell.com
info@macintyrepurcell.com

Printed and bound in Canada by Rapido Books

Cover design: Denis Cunningham
Book design: Gwen North
Author photo, back cover: Heidi Jirotka

Library and Archives Canada Cataloguing in Publication

Title: Forerunners : harbingers of death in Nova Scotia / Vernon Oickle.
Names: Oickle, Vernon, 1961- author.
Identifiers: Canadiana 20230473687 | ISBN 9781772761795 (softcover)
Subjects: LCSH: Omens—Nova Scotia—Anecdotes. | LCSH: Death—Nova
    Scotia—Anecdotes. | LCSH: Death—Nova Scotia—Miscellanea.
Classification: LCC BF1777 .O33 2023 | DDC 133.3/3409716—dc23

ISBN: 978-1-77276-180-1

MacIntyre Purcell Publishing Inc. would like to acknowledge the financial
support of the Government of Canada and the Nova Scotia Department of
Tourism, Culture and Heritage.

Dedication

This book is dedicated to the memory of
my mother, Viola, and grandmother, Pearl.
These two women inspired and influenced
my life-long fascination with forerunners.

The boundaries which divide
Life from Death are at best
shadowy and vague. Who shall
say where the one ends, and
where the other begins?

— Edgar Allan Poe

Table of Contents

What Is a Forerunner?

Some of the most common themes in Nova Scotia folklore are signs and omens of death. Forerunners appear not only in the ghost stories told around campfires late at night, they also occur in our literature and song. Intuition means paying attention to the smallest of detail, because in those details sometimes the crumbs of the future can be revealed.

Forerunners can take many forms and always present themselves to the receiver without warning but always leave a sense of foreboding and dread in their wake. The warnings can take the shape of an animal, such as a large black dog, or they can be a subtle incident such as a framed picture falling from the wall and shattering to pieces, or a window slamming shut for no visible reason.

Forerunners can also be a sound like a bell tolling in the distance that no one else in your proximity can hear. It can be three loud knocks on your door or window or from somewhere within the house. And you can receive a forerunner while you're awake or in your dreams. Only you know the seriousness of what has been revealed.

Signs of death can also be less subtle. For instance, when a bird slams into a window and dies, it can mean that someone you know will die in less than three days. To take this belief a step further, it is said that if a bird gets into your house, then it's a sign that someone in the house is about to die.

Imminent tragedy

These signs and omens are sent to us as a warning in an effort to prepare us for an imminent tragedy. They are still taken seriously, especially by those of us raised by parents and grandparents who would have been exposed to this oral history. These superstitions remain embedded in our culture, part of who we are.

Of all of the omens of death that exist in many of our communities, none are taken more seriously or leave such a deep-seeded sense of foreboding and heart-wrenching dread than forerunners. Forerunners can also be a voice, one of the most common of which comes in the form of someone whispering your name in your ear even though no one else is present.

Forerunners can take the shape of another person, usually a black, shadowy figure and often without any distinguishable facial features leaving one to wonder who — or what — it was.

Dr. Helen Creighton, the grande dame of Nova Scotia folklore and the inspiration to a legion of fans, describes forerunners "as warnings of something about to happen." She literally collected hundreds of examples of forerunners in her books. In fact, her book *Bluenose Ghosts* suggests that forerunners may indeed be the most common supernatural event to occur in Nova Scotia.

Forerunners, then, are an important part of Nova Scotia's oral folklore and have their foundation in what is a very real phenomenon. Many people have experienced them and some who do not believe in ghosts, seemingly have no hesitation believing in forerunners. This is a book about paying attention and listening (not dismissing) those voices and images that are part of all of our lives.

Dying is an art, like everything else.

— Sylvia Plath

From the Author – A Personal Story

From 1980 to 1982, I studied journalism in Lethbridge, Alberta, and the incident in question happened on a bitterly cold evening in January 1981.

I lived with several other college students in a large, rambling, three-storey, century-old home with what we charitably called a whole lot of character. It was Saturday night and all my friends had gone out for the evening. For some reason, I decided to stay home.

From where I sat in the living room watching television, I could see directly into the front yard through a large, bay window that spanned the front of the house. The window offered a view of the winding cement walkway that made its way through the yard and led to a wrought-iron fence flanked by a tall hedge.

At around 11 o'clock, I happened to glance out the window and saw a tall, broad-shouldered man dressed in a long, black overcoat and a wide-brimmed hat pass through the front gate. He came up the walkway and went around the side of the house to the back door.

I was sure we weren't expecting anyone that night so I thought that perhaps it was David, the homeowner and landlord, coming for a surprise inspection. He often did that, especially on Friday or Saturday nights, when he thought his tenants might be holding a party and he wanted to make sure things were not getting out of hand.

As I sat and watched the television across the room, fully expecting David to unlock the door and come inside from the cold, it suddenly struck me that I hadn't heard his footsteps on the back stairs.

If he had gone back out through the front gate, I would surely have seen him but I was sure he had not done that, and that reality set my nerves tingling. The appearance of the man in black began to make me feel uncomfortable, and I immediately experienced a strong sense of foreboding, as if something terrible was about to happen.

Hurrying to the back door, I peeked out through the frosted window expecting to see someone standing there waiting to be invited in. I wondered if there was someone out there without a key, but why would they not have knocked?

When I did open the door, no one was there. I stepped out into the cold night air onto the large, wraparound verandah, and looked around the back of the house.

Again, I saw no one.

Glancing to the ground dusted with a fresh layer of light snow, I could see there were no footprints.

I shivered as an icy wave of fear washed over me.

What was going on here?

I hurried back inside the house and slammed the door behind me. Once inside, I felt like my world was closing in on me. I knew there had been something unusual about the man I had seen, but I could not explain what it was or where he had gone.

Shaken and questioning what I had just experienced, I turned off the television and went to bed. I did not sleep well that night.

Meanwhile, back home

The next night, as I did every two weeks, I phoned my parents to see how things were going back home in Liverpool. My mother, who seemed to have a sixth sense about these things, immediately detected something was wrong and asked if everything was okay.

I had not planned to tell her about my experience from the night before because I did not want her to worry, so I hesitated. I finally asked her if everyone was all right and she stalled with her answer. As I knew she would, she could sense something was bothering me and wondered why I would ask such a question. I then told her about my unexplained visitor.

"When did this happen?" she asked when I finished my story.

"Last night," I told her.

"What time?"

"About 11 o'clock," I answered.

I could tell by her sudden silence that something, indeed, was bothering her too. She then told me that on the previous evening when I had seen the mysterious man, at exactly the same time (two o'clock in the morning in Nova Scotia), my parents were awakened by my sister's screams from the next bedroom.

Rushing to investigate the ruckus, they found my sister in tears sitting up in bed and shaking like a leaf in a violent windstorm. When she finally calmed down, she told them that she had been sleeping but was suddenly awakened with the feeling that some-one had entered the room.

At first, she thought it must have been either my mother or father or a friend who had been staying over that night and was sleeping in another room. When she opened her eyes, however, she told my parents that she was horrified to see a large man dressed in a long black overcoat and wide-brimmed hat standing at the foot of her bed looking down at her.

She said the man disappeared when she screamed, but his appearance left her shaken to the bone and feeling a terrible sense of grief and loss.

Putting the two stories together, my mother became convinced that something bad was about to happen to someone we knew. She felt the appearance of the man in black was a sign and she insisted that someone in the family was going to die.

The next day an uncle passed away.

You might think all of this is a coincidence, but my mother was convinced that what my sister and I had seen that night had been our uncle's forerunner coming to warn us that we should be ready for an impending tragedy.

Perhaps it was all a coincidence but like my mother, I don't think so. For me, this incident confirmed that forerunners are very real.

Life is like a garden. Perfect moments can be had, but not preserved, except in memory.

— Leonard Nimoy

Wave Goodbye

Accounts of forerunners, omens of death and premonitions can be found going back through the annals of Nova Scotia's storied history. This tale comes from the picturesque and historic port community of Port Medway, Queens County.

Since the arrival of the settlers in the 1760s, the port has seen the comings and goings of many vessels of various types and sizes, everything from large merchant vessels to small fishing boats. All have been built and sailed from this port. The intertwined life of the sea, souls and ships has left a legacy of marine tales that have been passed on from one generation to the next.

This one comes to us from the mid 1920s and is shared by Liverpool historian Kathleen Stitt.

There was a sailing ship from the Port under the command of Captain McConnell, an experienced man of the sea. It was said he had seen it all: ships becalmed for want of a good breeze, ships tossed by ocean waves during a fierce gale, and ships racing the waves in perfect weather.

Captain McConnell knew the dangers and the rewards of life lived on the ocean.

Over his many years, he had taken hundreds of sailors under his command. He'd seen old sea dogs who knew the wind and the waves almost as well as he did as well as the first-time adventurer wanting to seek his fortune on the ocean. Captain McConnell had also seen men at their bravest, helping a fellow sailor in time of need and the terror in their eyes when the ocean showed her cruelty.

On this particular day, he was preparing to go on another voyage, one he thought should be very easy compared to some of the sails he had undertaken. A quick run to a nearby port with a load of timber and back again sounded pretty easy to him. He had hired his crew and was preparing to sail on the morning tide. About dawn, a young sailor came to the captain and said he had a bad feeling about this trip.

The sailor told the captain that the night before he had dreamt that he would not return from the trip. Would the captain release him from his commitment to sail, he asked timidly?

The old captain understood the sailor's reluctance and if he had another sailor available to take his place, he would have surely released the young man. As it was, however, the ship was undermanned and he could spare no one without a replacement.

The young man continued to protest that he feared going to sea on this trip. His fear was palpable.

Getting no satisfaction from the captain the young man decided to make a run for it. He jumped off the ship and ran down the wharf in hopes of avoiding the trip. In turn, the captain sent a few men to stop the fledgling sailor and bring him back to the boat.

The captain tried to calm the young man.

"Son," he cautioned, trying to steady the novice sailor. "We will be all right. You have been to sea before. You are letting fear control you. Okay men," the captain ordered, "cast off the lines and let's get going."

A clear day

It was a beautiful day in the harbour, both wind and tide were in the ship's favour. The sky was clear. As the ship and crew settled into the routine of the day, the young man began to settle himself. Perhaps he was just letting his fear and imagination get the best of him.

A short time into the trip he calmed his nerves and joined his crewmates in the many tasks that needed to be done on a sailing ship. About four hours into the cruise and it was smooth sailing. By now, the young man was more at ease and was standing on deck when his fate finally caught up with him.

Later, back in port, his shipmates reported a huge, rogue wave suddenly formed and crashed over the deck without warning. There was little time to brace himself. The young man lost his balance and was sucked overboard. The men quickly began a search. For several hours, the crew searched and searched but there was no sign of the sailor.

The young man was gone, lost to an unforgiving sea, just as he had dreamed the night before.

In a subsequent newspaper story about the tragedy, one of the crew described the event this way: "It was as if the wave formed a giant hand and grabbed the sailor and pulled him into the embrace of the cold, cruel ocean. The sea immediately calmed, and the rest of the voyage was uneventful."

Did the young sailor dream of his own death?

Was the dream an omen or warning?

Or was it just another sad tale of a sailor lost at sea?

The universe moves in mysterious ways.

One never knows the ending.
One has to die to know
exactly what happens after
death. Although Catholics
have their hopes.

— Alfred Hitchcock

That Sinking Feeling

In the seaside hamlet of Liverpool on Nova Scotia's South Shore, you'll find an interesting monument that speaks to the town's historic and tragic connection to the unforgiving Atlantic. More about that history later on as this is a story that has become the stuff of local legend.

The story is best conveyed by local resident, Linda Moulton, who tells of the night her grandmother received an unannounced visitor to her front door.

Linda's grandmother, Elsie Jollimore, was born in 1904 in Liverpool and she remembers as a child her grandmother telling her the story of her own father's passing.

"Allen Jollimore was my grandmother's father," Linda begins. "He and his son, Fred Jollimore, were both crewmembers of the beam trawler *Jutland*. My grandmother Elsie was still living at home with her parents, Allen and Mary. She was 16 years of age at the time. Allen and Fred were both out at sea on the *Jutland* when this story takes place."

All of a sudden, through the night of March 11, 1920, there was a banging at the front door, Linda recalls her grandmother telling her.

"My great grandmother Mary was alarmed and got up to investigate. When she opened the door, her husband Allen was standing there and he was all wet. Water was dripping off of him. In a word, he was drenched."

I love you

Linda continues, "As my great grandfather looked at his wife, he said, 'You won't be seeing me for a long time. I just wanted to come back to tell you I love you.' Then he turned around and walked away."

Being confused by what was going on, Mary went back to bed thinking she must have dreamt this. Later the next day, however, she received word that the *Jutland* had gone down along with all 21 souls on board, and that included her husband and son.

"My grandmother told me that her mother went to bed that night with her dark hair but woke up the next morning and it was white," Linda says. "They called the doctor to come to the house and check on her and he said it was probably the shock of losing her husband and son."

Elsie, Linda's grandmother, was a teenager when she lost her father. "She told me that she continued to miss him terribly over the years. She was always telling the story to family members of the loss of her father and how he came to the house that night to say his final goodbye to his wife."

True or not true, this is the stuff of local legend.

Jutland was a Canadian beam trawler based out of Liverpool, Nova Scotia. Built in 1918 by the Boehner Bros., she was owned by LaHave Fishing Company.

On March 10, 1920, *Jutland* left Halifax, Nova Scotia, with a crew of 21 heading to the Western Bank fishing grounds. On the morning of March 11, the Halifax steam trawler *Lemberg* discovered two dories approximately 160 kilometers (86 nautical miles) southeast of Halifax.

Both dories were damaged and full of water. The body of John R. Ellison, a mate of the *Jutland*, was discovered aboard one of the dories. The bodies of the 20 other crewmembers were never recovered.

Various theories on what happened to *Jutland* have been offered up over the years, from an explosion to a collision, but a definitive conclusion has never been rendered. Whether the *Jutland* struck a floating mine or an unheralded storm took her to the bottom, is not known so the tragedy will forever remain a mystery.

In honour of those who perished on the beam trawler *Jutland*, two anchors that had been salvaged by the *Jutland* on the trip just before her last in 1920, comprise a memorial that can be found in a historic cemetery in Liverpool.

It was decreed that the anchors were a fitting gravestone for the crew that were lost with the ship. In 1921, these anchors, along with an inscribed stone, were mounted in the Old Burial

Ground Cemetery on Main Street, Liverpool, as a memorial to the lost 21 crewmembers.

The memorial includes the pair of crossed anchors that guard a marble table bearing the inscription, "God's Mercy-Our Hope," placed there as a symbol of hope that their souls were resting in eternal peace.

The connections we make in the course of a life — maybe that's what heaven is.

— Fred Rogers

The Baddeck Forerunner

Baddeck is a quaint village located in northeastern Nova Scotia situated almost dead-center of Cape Breton Island. It is also the adopted hometown of the inventor of the telephone, Alexander Graham Bell, and where Bell chose as his resting place for him and his wife, Mabel.

Its storied history stretches back many centuries to the region's first inhabitants, the Mi'kmaq, and to the early settlers, namely the French and English. It is no surprise then that Baddeck has had its fair share of tales from the world of the paranormal, including one of Cape Breton Island's most famous forerunner stories.

Today, as you head to Baddeck from Margaree, you are fortunate to travel along the modern roads and highways of the 21st century. This, of course, was not always the case. Matter of fact, before modern roads were built getting to Baddeck involved navigating poorly maintained roads, which were actually little more than oxen paths, hardly suitable for carriage trips. One can sympathize with the early doctors trying to attend to the patients under their care, especially for doctors with large practices in rural regions.

This legendary story involves one of those physicians who often left his Baddeck home base and travelled to settlements near and far over sometimes deplorable trails to take care of the sick and injured. The story goes that one dark night the doctor was returning home from one of his sick calls when all of a sudden his horse immediately came to a halt and no amount of encouragement or inducement could make the animal move.

Bright light

As the doctor continued to coax his horse into moving forward, he observed a bright light moving methodically toward him. Then, suddenly, there appeared within the light the distinct outline of a human face, which revealed a radiance so beautiful that the doctor could not resist staring at it.

At first the brilliance of the light shone so brightly he had to squint his eyes, but within minutes the face began to fade and grow dimmer until it eventually disappeared into the ball of light in which it appeared, before fading away into complete darkness.

So impressed was the doctor that despite the late hour upon which he arrived home, he awoke his wife from her sleep after midnight and told her about his unusual encounter with the light and glowing face. It is said that the doctor's wife, being a God-fearing woman, cautioned her husband's excitement pointing out that the sighting could have been a vision of a divine nature, or it could have been his imagination brought on by his fatigue.

Considering his wife's cautionary observation, the doctor lay awake for the remainder of the night thinking about what he had seen. He was convinced that he had not imagined the vision and in fact the glowing vision was an encounter with the supernatural.

As the days passed and memories of the mysterious event faded into the background, the doctor went about his business tending to his patients throughout the region until a week later tragic news reached his Baddeck office.

He was summoned to the scene of a mishap on the same road the doctor had travelled days earlier. A man, along with the man's wife and child, were all ejected from their small carriage when one of its wheels came off. It was the very same spot where the doctor's horse had stopped and he had seen the face in the light days earlier.

He first went to check on the man's wife where he found her moaning and laying in the rocky path. She was injured but would survive. Next, he examined the man who was also sprawled on the ground and suffering. While he was in pain, the man was still alive at least.

Lastly, when he picked up the child that had been laying perfectly still on the ground, the doctor knew immediately that the child had died from the injuries it had sustained in the accident. He also recognized the child's face as the one he had seen in the ball of light a week earlier.

Death, the only immortal who treats us all alike, whose pity and whose peace and whose refuge are for all the soiled and the pure, the rich and the poor, the loved and the unloved.

— Mark Twain

When the Clock Strikes 13

For many Nova Scotians, forerunners and omens of death are part of their cultural foundation, with such superstitions and legends being considered normal occurrences.

So, like thousands of others who grew up with such engrained beliefs and traditions stemming from their childhoods, both Dianne and Brian Nowe who reside in Bridgewater, Nova Scotia, embrace their shared heritage.

"I have always been a believer," says Dianne. "It's hard not to accept that these things are real when you've been exposed to them your entire life, as we have been. It becomes so common that you just accept them."

While she's heard many stories over the years of people receiving warnings of death from forerunners, she says it wasn't until 2021 that a personal incident not only removed any lingering doubt she may have had about such things but also left her shaken to her core.

"It's one thing to say you believe in such phenomena because of the stories you've grown up with, but it's a totally different thing when something happens to you. It changes your whole perspective."

In 2021, as the COVID-19 pandemic was just beginning to embrace the globe, Dianne recalls sitting in her living room one afternoon when all of a sudden a "very loud" thud startled her. She knew right away that a bird had hit the window.

"The bang was so loud that it left me shivering as ice chills ran up my spine. I knew right away what it meant. I knew that a bird hitting a window was a sign of death and that someone close to me was going to die."

She also knew not to dismiss such warnings and that she should take heed.

"I knew enough to know that I could sense something was very wrong," she adds. "It gave me a very bad feeling."

And sure enough, something was, indeed, about to go wrong. The following Wednesday Dianne received word that her mother had suddenly died.

"It was a shock," she says, fighting back the raw emotion that easily comes to the surface when she talks about her mother. "But I had been warned and I had been waiting for the bad news. I just never expected it would be my mom because she wasn't sick."

Not easy to forget

Dianne's husband, Brian, agrees that such experiences that deal with omens of death are not so easily forgotten. In fact, now at age 77, he still vividly recalls events from when he was ten years old.

Growing up in Bayport, a small fishing village located in Lunenburg County, Brian explains that his father worked in the boating industry in Toronto and was often gone for extended periods of time. In those days, he says, it was usually necessary for people to travel to places like Ontario to get good jobs to support their family.

Brian also remembers all his sisters and brothers getting very excited each time their father was due to come home for a visit; this particular visit was going to be even extra special as they were going to be celebrating his father's birthday.

While the journey from Toronto to Bayport — located on the outskirts of the town of Lunenburg — in the 1950s took several days by motor vehicle, it was was more economical to travel by car than by plane or train. With few exceptions, most easterners choose that mode of transportation to make the long journey home several times a year. Brian explains his father was travelling home in his uncle's car as he had done on many other occasions.

"It was on the night that my father was supposed to arrive home, I will never forget it for as long as I live. The whole family was gathered at our house waiting for him to come home when we heard it — all of us. We heard the clock chime 13 times."

Not possible? Perhaps.

However, even though Brian admits that he knows it sounds odd, the whole family agreed that the clock had chimed 13 times.

"Now, since I was only ten years old at the time, I may not have fully understood the significance of that extra chime, but as the events unfolded that night, we all came to realize that it had been a warning."

It had been a warning

Later that night, as they awaited his father's arrival, the family received word that there had been a terrible car accident just outside of Lunenburg and they were told that his father had been killed not far from the village. He would never make it home to celebrate his birthday.

Brian says they later learned that while his father was driving home from Lunenburg, he noticed that another car had left the road and was partially submerged in the cold water of the LaHave River. Doing what any good Samaritan would do, his father stopped and helped the occupants from that vehicle to get to safety.

Once those people were safe and emergency crews had arrived, Brian's father got in his own car again and continued the journey home. However, tragedy struck when minutes later his car left the road and he was killed.

Brian agrees there are lots of questions surrounding the events of that evening. What if his father had not stopped to help those people in the earlier accident? Would he have made it home? Possibly, but that's a question that can never be answered.

The other burning question for Brian and the other family members was the number of times the clock chimed. Was the extra 13th chime a warning of this father's impending death? Maybe it could be simply explained as the clock malfunctioning but Brian says he doesn't think so as no one ever heard that extra chime before or after his father's accident.

No, Brian believes the extra chime was something more than a malfunctioning clock.

"It was a warning," he says. "I've always believed that for whatever reason, we received notice that my father was not going to make it home that night. There really is no other explanation."

Think about it. When was the last time you ever heard a clock strike 13?

Death is something inevitable. When a man has done what he considers to be his duty to his people and his country, he can rest in peace.

— Nelson Mandela

A Gift or a Curse

Some people seem to have a dark cloud that follows them no matter where they go.

For Sheri Roy of Liverpool, Nova Scotia, that dark cloud is sometimes followed by the death of someone she loves or at least leads to a very serious incident that could be life-threatening to someone close to her.

But even though she admits that she probably has more of these experiences than most people, she takes it all in stride, accepting that she has inherited the same "gift" that her late mother, Linda, possessed. Although, she adds, sometimes she wonders if it isn't more of a curse.

"Mom saw these things all the time," Sheri says, recalling her mother's sense of intuition that often foretold of an impending tragedy.

"It was strong with her throughout her whole life; so strong that I remember her talking about something that happened to her when she was younger and she said she had this feeling for two weeks leading up to the assignation of JFK (on November 22, 1963). She always said the feelings were so intense that she wasn't really surprised when it actually happened."

Sheri also remembers her mother talking about an event that occurred in September 1979.

"I was still very young and on this particular day when mom came into my room to check on me, she was startled to see a man standing at the foot of my bed," she says, recalling the story her mother often told her about the event. "According to her, this man was just standing there, watching over me and mom always said she knew it was a forerunner. She didn't know who was going to die, but she knew someone was."

A short while later, on September 12, 1979, just a day after her mother's birthday, the family received word that her mother's brother, Lionel, had been killed in a terrible car accident.

"Mom took the news of his death very hard," Sheri says. "She was absolutely convinced without a doubt that even though she was not able to identify him, the man she had seen standing over my bed was the forerunner of her brother."

In light of her mother's abilities, it only stands to reason that Sheri would also experience such phenomena. For instance, she says, in 2001 before the death of a close friend, she saw "someone" in her kitchen on three or four different occasions.

"It was a warning," she insists. "It was a warning that someone was going to die and within a few days, I lost a really close friend."

Who was that?

By June 2005, Sheri had been holding down a full-time job and was married with two young children — two boys ages two and five. Her mother often helped take care of the children while she was at work.

Sheri recalls the day in June when, following a busy day on the job, she was driving into her parents' driveway as she always did to pick up her boys, only this time she was startled to see someone quickly come out from around the side of her dad's garage and then vanish. The person moved quickly, but Sheri says she thought right away that it must have been her mother as she is certain it looked like a female figure. She soon discovered that her mother had not been anywhere near the garage.

So, if it hadn't been her mother and no one else had seen a woman near the garage that day then who was it?

"Honestly," Sheri admits with a shrug, "I have no idea but the whole thing left me feeling unsettled because I knew what these things can mean. The next day, when I told the people I worked with about what I had seen, they all agreed that I had seen a forerunner—and truthfully, that's what I was thinking too. Just based upon on how unsettled I felt after I saw the figure, I knew it was something out of the ordinary."

Later that month, Sheri received confirmation that, indeed, the figure had been a forerunner when she got a call telling her that there had been a terrible accident involving her husband, Travis, and a second driver, a woman, who had driven her vehicle head-first into Travis' truck.

"It was June 22 and the accident happened around 5 a.m. that day when the woman crossed the road into Travis' lane and hit him front on. Travis wasn't seriously injured but the woman later died in hospital."

In hindsight Sheri says she reached the conclusion that the female figure she had seen at her parents' garage earlier that month, was actually the forerunner of the woman involved in her husband's accident.

Sheri says she had grown used to these occurrences. Pointing back to an incident that happened on June 7, 2003, she remembers the events of that morning very well, explaining that while she was busy vacuuming the floors, she observed a man walking down the hallway in her house from the living room to the bedrooms. And that was strange, she adds, because she was alone in the house at the time.

Not afraid

"These things don't usually scare me because they happen fairly often," she explains, but seeing the sight of a man in the hallway left her feeling unnerved.

Again, like all of these incidents, she could not clearly see the man's face so she could not identify who it was but she is certain it was a man.

"Then, a day or so later, we received word that my father-in-law had died without warning of a massive heart attack," she says, adding that his death was a major surprise because he was only 52 years old at that time.

"I knew it was going to be something major. I just knew it

because of that man I had seen walking in the hallway. Thinking back on the incident, I believe it must have been my father-in-law. He was there as a warning. ... He was telling me to be ready. I feel that's what it was and it all made sense to me."

Despite all of these tragic happenings and eventual bad news, the warnings keep on coming and Sheri relates the events surrounding December 15, 2009, to illustrate just how receptive she is to such phenomena.

More bad news

As a truck driver, Sheri says she accepts that Travis faces certain risks every time he's on the road and she points out that he's had way more than his fair share of close calls over the years. One particular dark, rainy night in December 2009 she says he came very close again to meeting his demise.

"I later learned that the accident happened around 10 p.m. that night when the second vehicle swerved into the wrong lane and hit Travis' truck head on," she explains. "The man driving that vehicle died instantly but thankfully Travis wasn't seriously hurt."

Despite the initial shock of hearing about the accident and being seriously worried about her husband, Sheri admits she was not at all surprised to receive word about the accident because she was expecting something tragic to happen.

"You see," she begins "just before I received the call about the accident, I saw a man standing in the middle of my living room and even though he was only there for a few seconds before he vanished, he was there long enough for me to know that it was a warning and I knew whatever was going to happen, it was not going to good."

Some people may consider it a curse to be receptive to such things, but Sheri says over the years she has learned to take them all in stride.

"I can honestly say these things do not scare me," she explains matter-of-factly. "But they always leave me puzzled and worried about what's going to happen. I always have questions — who's going to die now? Is it going to be someone in the family? Or a close friend?"

That's always the hard part of receiving such warnings — they leave you worrying as to what tragedy is coming your way.

Death is nature's way of saying,
'Your table is ready.'

— Robin Williams

Knock. Knock. Who's There?

It is actually three knocks on a door, window or sometimes even a wall that is a forerunner or precursor of impending death. More precisely if the source of that sound cannot be located, then it means death will come to someone close to you. Typically, those three knocks come within a three-day window in which that death is said to occur.

Bernice Mason of Cape Breton not only believes in such paranormal phenomena, but she experienced it firsthand. And not just once but at least four times.

"I guess I must be just one of those special people," she says, noting that she had her first encounter with the knocking forerunner when she was 17 years of age. "It looks like my mother and I shared the same gift when it came to such things."

Number one

The events took place many years ago on a late Saturday afternoon, recalls the woman who celebrated her 89th birthday in September 2022. She remembers the beans were baking in the oven in preparation for the traditional Saturday supper and the family was keeping busy while they waited.

"We were all in the kitchen," Bernice begins. "There were five us there that day. As it was a very cold afternoon, Mother and I were sitting beside the big woodstove we had for cooking and for also heating the house. It was the only heating source we had in those days so it was customary to gather in the kitchen, which was always the warmest room in the house. Mother was knitting some mittens for the men to wear when they went hunting or working on the boats. I was doing some darning that Mother had asked me to help her with."

At the same time, her father, her older brother, Greg, and a friend of the family who had become a regular visitor at the home every Saturday for supper, were playing cards at the kitchen table.

"If this old memory serves me correctly, I believe they were playing cribbage," she laughs. "It was my father's favourite game. He and the others would play for hours every Saturday afternoon, unless there was work to be done. Then the work was always done first."

The other thing Bernice recalls was that the men were waiting for a fourth player to show up. Typically, that would be her uncle

Bobby, her mother's younger brother.

"Bobby was never on time, so the others started without him," she explained. "Uncle Bobby would join in when he got there, whenever that was. Sometimes, he could be a couple hours late. He was not very reliable that way."

Bernice says the men had been playing for about an hour and a half when the strange event happened.

"They were playing and Mother and I were busy doing our work when all of sudden I heard three loud knocks on the back door that led right into the kitchen. Mother and I just looked at each other and, assuming that it was Uncle Bob we went back to our work; then a few minutes later, when we heard the three knocks a second time."

She says her mother asked if one of the men was going to tell Bobby to come in, as the door was not locked.

"'What are you talking about?' my brother asked Mother. And she promptly told him that he should tell Uncle Bobby to come in because he has been knocking at the door."

When her brother told her that they had not heard anything she replied, "Well, he has been knocking because your sister and I heard it."

Almost as if to prove the point, Bernice remembers her mother getting up and going to the door where she expected to find her brother Bob standing there.

"Only, he wasn't there," she says, adding, "Actually, there was no one there. Mother even called out for Uncle Bobby but no one answered."

Odd, she recalls her mother saying, confirming that Bernice had indeed heard the knocks.

"I most assuredly did, I told my mother. It was as clear as clear as can be. I heard it. Mother heard it but none of the men heard it even though the door was right next to the table where they were playing cards."

The unsettling part came two days later when her uncle Bob did come knocking at the kitchen door. Only this time he wasn't coming to play a friendly game of cards; he was coming to tell Bernice's mother that her father — "my grandfather" — had just died about an hour earlier.

"He told Mother he didn't know what happened but said that when Papa went to get up from his chair, he just keeled over and then he was gone," she recalls. "It was such a shock for everyone because I don't remember that man ever being sick a single day in his life."

Bernice is convinced that what she and her mother had experienced that Saturday afternoon before her grandfather died was, in fact, death coming to warn them to be ready for an impending tragedy.

"As Mother and I had discussed many times over the years, we should have known something strange was going to happen because in hindsight we should have realized that things were a little off when Uncle Bobby hadn't just opened the door and walked right into the house like he had done so many times before," she says.

"You're always left with questions," Bernice says, pointing out that her second encounter with a forerunner came when she was 35, many years after her mother and father had died and she was a married woman with four children of her own.

KNOCK. KNOCK. WHO'S THERE?

Number two

"If you believe in these things like I do, then you know how to recognize the signs right away and I knew that Uncle Bobby was going to die the night before it actually happened," she says, recalling the events of decades earlier when she was helping her youngest daughter complete her homework.

"It was October 30, the night before Halloween," she begins. "Sarah and I were at the kitchen table where she was working on her math homework. We were both concentrating on what she was doing when we heard these three loud taps on the kitchen window located just in front of the table. We both jumped because it scared us half to death."

Bernice says she didn't say anything to her daughter about the knocks, but she immediately got up from the table and looked outside, scanning the yard to see if anyone was there.

"I couldn't see anyone and then I asked Sarah if she heard anything. Yes, she said. She had heard the same thing."

Not wanting to scare her daughter, Bernice didn't tell her that three knocks meant that someone was going to die; instead she reassured her that no one was outside and the knocking must have been the wind.

"I knew it wasn't the wind," says Bernice. "It wasn't blowing all that hard and besides the knocks were very loud and they came very quickly. There was no doubt, though, that it was three knocks, which I knew in my heart that it meant it was a forerunner."

And sure enough, she received word the next morning that her uncle had died the night before.

"He hadn't been well for a number of years," she recalls. "He had prostate cancer and it spread throughout his whole body. He suffered for a long time so I wasn't really surprised when I heard he had died, but it did prove to me that it was his forerunner that Sarah and I heard knocking at our kitchen window the night before. I am sure of that."

Number three

Her third encounter with a forerunner occurred thirteen years ago when she was sitting in her favourite living room chair watching her favourite television shows, *Jeopardy* and *Wheel of Fortune*. They were also her husband's favourite shows and it was their evening ritual to watch them together, but he had been dead now for several years at that point.

"Murray was very smart. He didn't get all the answers on *Jeopardy* but he sure did get a lot of them. I could not keep up with him, but it was fun trying," she says fondly. "After he died, I kept watching the shows but the evenings were never the same without him."

On this particular evening, Bernice says *Wheel of Fortune* had just ended and she was thinking it was soon time for her to turn in for the night.

"I wasn't thinking about anything really, then all of sudden I hear these three very distinct knocking sounds and I wondered who would be coming to my house at that hour. It was definitely somebody knocking and it was coming from somewhere in the house. I went and looked around everywhere, but I couldn't see anyone or anything so, just like before, I assumed this was another sign. It kind of scared me and I thought maybe I should phone someone to come over and check things out, but I decided not to bother anyone."

Sure enough it certainly was a sign as the next morning her oldest daughter, Margaret (Margie), who lived just five minutes away with her own family, came to deliver the news that Bernice's brother, Greg, had died the night before in his sleep.

"Greg's son told Margie he didn't suffer or anything. He just went to sleep the night before and never woke up." She pauses, gathers her thoughts, and continues, "Funny how that happens sometimes, with no warning or anything, but I am glad he didn't suffer. He was the last of my immediate family except for me."

Number four

Bernice had one more encounter with a forerunner just over three years ago. This incident involved her cousin, Louise, who lived in Hamilton, Ontario. Even though she and Louise had not seen each other many years, they kept in touch, exchanging letters and cards on special occasions and a yearly phone call over the Christmas holidays.

"We were only two years apart in age — I was the oldest — and so we were pretty close to each other growing up," she says, adding that she and Louise were actually more like sisters than cousins. "Our fathers were brothers, so our families were always visiting with each other and it was only natural that we would be close."

Bernice and Louise moved on with their own lives, getting married, having children and, in Louise's case, moving away with her husband to Hamilton for a job. "I always felt we had this special connection and I believe that's why she reached out to me one last time just before she died."

As with her previous experiences with forerunners, Bernice says she wasn't thinking about anything death related at the time the event occurred. "These things always just happen out of the blue. It's not like you sit around waiting for a forerunner to show up."

She recalls the afternoon that she's convinced Louise visited her as a warning to be prepared that something was going to happen. Bernice explains she was actually on the phone talking to her daughter Sarah, who was working in Halifax at the time.

"She had been on an interview for a new job that morning and she called to tell me she thought it went well and that she believed she would get it," says Bernice. "We had just begun talking when suddenly I heard three loud knocks at the front door so I told Sarah to hang on for a minute until I checked to see who was there."

Putting the phone on the table, Bernice says she went to the front door but no one was there. She felt her heart sink because she says she knew right away what this meant.

"I went back to the phone and told Sarah what had happened. By this time, all my children had heard all about my stories with forerunners and such things, so we both wondered what was going to happen."

Later that afternoon, she found out what was going to happen when she received a phone call from Louise's son telling her that his mother had died that afternoon.

"When I thought about it after the news sunk in, I remembered that whenever Louise and her family came home for a visit, they always travelled the front door and Louise always knocked before coming in, even though I would always jokingly tell her she didn't have to knock."

Did Louise reach out to her one last time before her death?

Bernice is absolutely convinced she did. "Oh, I know it was Louise, just like I knew it was the others all those years earlier. She wanted to tell me not to worry, that she was going to be all right."

No one wants to die. Even people who want to go to heaven don't want to die to get there. And yet, death is the destination we all share. No one has ever escaped it, and that is how it should be, because death is very likely the single best invention of life. It's life's change agent. It clears out the old to make way for the new.

— Steve Jobs

Jasper and Grinch

O ne of the greatest misconceptions people have about forerunners is that they believe the warning has to take the shape of a person but that is not always the case.

In fact, forerunners can come in the form of an animal or bird. As we have already learned, they can also be a sound, such as knocking at a door, window or wall, or a bell tolling that no one else other than you can hear. A forerunner can also be a smell, a dream or a feeling, or it can be someone whispering your name in your ear even though you are alone.

For Gwennie Weaver of Spectacle Lake, Lunenburg County, that warning to her family came in a "feeling." It was a feeling so intense and so profound that Gwennie says it impacted her entire life and future.

Born in Halifax, Gwennie moved to Lunenburg with her husband, Terry, in the 1960s and eventually they settled in the Spectacle Lake area where they raised their only child, a son, Shane. Everything was going well until June 2003 when she says her life was forever changed.

Terry came from a long and proud line of fishers who spent their lives at sea. Her husband loved the water, and by 2003 Terry had landed a good job on board the *Atlantic Leader*, a freezer trawler in the Clearwater fleet.

Then, after the second to the last trip that Terry ever made on the vessel, something happened and everything changed.

"We were chatting after he got home from that trip and he was telling me about the feeling he suddenly had while he was crawling into his bunk a few nights earlier," she says. "For some reason he could not explain he told me that he experienced the presence of his deceased dog, Jasper, standing beside the bunk. He said the feeling was so intense and that it left him shaken. He had never experienced anything like it before."

Later, that same evening, she says, she had a dream that also involved the family's two deceased dogs, Jasper and Grinch. In that dream, she was searching for the two pets on Bluenose Drive and Montague Street in the Town of Lunenburg.

"After all of that, Terry became concerned about what it could mean," she says.

"Growing up in Nova Scotia, I had heard about warnings of death and things like forerunners, but honestly I never really thought about it very much because I had never personally experienced anything like that. But all of these 'signs' meant something to Terry and it really bothered him, so much so that he began to have reservations about getting back on the boat for another trip."

A gut feeling

"He said he had a 'gut feeling' that something wasn't right," says Gwennie. Being a life-long fisherman and understanding the profession comes with risks, he pushed aside his feelings and reservations, got back on the ship, and sailed off on another trip."

As Gwennie was able to keep in touch with Terry via the satellite phone when he was out to sea, they had several conversations over the next couple days.

"Every time I talked to him I could tell there was still apprehension in his voice. I could tell something wasn't right with him … that he wasn't his normal self," Gwennie says.

She remembers Terry called on Shane's 14th birthday but the call kept breaking up and it was hard to have a good conversation because of the bad connection.

"When Terry called me around 7 or 7:30 we talked and he said he just called because he wanted to hear my voice. I told him repeatedly that I loved him and that I was looking forward to seeing him when he came home."

Terry never came home and she never talked to him again. The deck boss on duty told Gwennie and the authorities an accident had happened around 11:30 p.m.

A freak accident

"They told me it was a freak accident in which the first mate hit the lever for the wrong rake. They said the rake came up and struck Terry, knocking him over the side," she says, the raw emotion that come with the loss of a loved one still audible in her voice. "They said it happened so fast that no one had a chance to grab him before he went over."

With a man overboard, the captain ordered an immediate stop and had the ship turn around. The crew were able to maintain visual contact with Terry for about five minutes and they could see him treading water. Then he disappeared into the waves and was gone. He was never found.

"It was a horrible, horrible night," says Gwennie. "When one of the gentlemen from the company's Lunenburg office came to my door at 2:30 in the morning, I knew right away that something terrible had happened to Terry. When they told me that he was lost overboard I went into shock and it took me a long time to recover, not that I ever really did. You never recover from something like that."

Lost at sea

While it was difficult to carry on without her husband, Gwennie says one of the hardest things about losing him at sea is that they never recovered his body. She says she takes some comfort in the fact that Terry did reach out to her in his own way in the days following the accident.

"It was a couple of days after Terry was lost that Shane and I awoke to the sound of someone chopping kindling in the back yard but there was no one there," she says. "I knew right away it was Terry because he loved to chop wood and I believe it was his way of reaching out to let me he was okay."

This was confirmation for Gwennie that there are things in the universe that one simply cannot explain, like the presence of our deceased dogs and the dreams.

It may be tempting to dismiss the signs as nothing more than old wives' tales but after what her family experienced, Gwennie believes such signs are much more than that.

Even death is not to be feared by
one who has lived wisely.

— Buddha

When Death Comes Knocking

As a child growing up in the seafaring town of Liverpool, Nova Scotia, Pam Miller was exposed to stories of the supernatural as the region was. Stories of ghosts, forerunners, premonitions, omens of death and other such phenomena were commonplace in her household.

"It was a different time back then. My mother, my grandmother, my whole family talked about seeing 'things.' They believed in forerunners and signs of death." And, she quickly adds, she believes them too.

"I've had many encounters with forerunners and omens of death, especially hearing three knocks," Pam says. "I heard three knocks before my mother died. I heard three knocks in the days leading up to my father's death and I heard three knocks just before my grandson died, so I know they are real."

It is a little unnerving when she hears these things, Pam admits, but mostly she's left wondering who's about die.

"It's hard when I hear it because I know what's coming," she says. "I know it's a warning and those warnings always come true, so I never dismiss it when it happens. I can't do anything about them, but I always brace myself for what is about to happen."

Forerunners are more than superstition, she insists.

"You'll know you've experienced a forerunner when you see one because of the way it leaves you feeling," she says. "It's just a very emotional experience because you know you've just received a sign that always leads to a death and *that* death is always of someone you know."

A visitor

Pam says she believes her most profound encounter occurred in 1994 and involved the mother of her husband, Reg.

"When Reg's mother got really sick back in 1994, she moved to Halifax because it was easier for her to get the care she needed," Pam recalls.

"She knew she was very ill, but she always told us that if at all possible she would come back to see Craig (their infant son) one more time before anything happened to her. Of course, as she got sicker, it became increasingly more difficult for her to travel, so she never did get that chance to visit us again before she died."

Not physically at least.

Between 9 and 9:30 on that autumn evening, Pam recalls

sitting in her living room and watching her mother-in-law come down the driveway and walk past the front of the house. While in most cases it's usually difficult or impossible to clearly distinguish the identity of a forerunner, in this particular case Pam says there is absolutely no doubt who it was.

"I knew it was Reg's mother and I knew right away what was going to happen," she says. "I knew it wasn't going be good so I immediately told Reg he should get ready for the phone to ring and, within minutes the phone rang. That's when we received word that his mother had just passed."

Forerunners are real, she says.

"I knew right away it was her in the driveway and she was coming to check on Craig one more time."

The truth I have been seeking —
this truth is Death. Yet Death is
also a seeker. Forever seeking me.
So we have met at last. And I am
prepared. I am at peace.

— Bruce Lee

Signs of Death Come in Threes

The number three plays a prominent role in Nova Scotia folklore.

There are many "old sayings" that revolve around threes, most prominently among them is the belief that three knocks to your door, window or walls without a source being readily identifiable, is a sign that death will occur within three days.

There's also the belief that bad luck runs in a string of three and that death in a family or community will often occur in threes. In some parts of Nova Scotia there's also the belief that seeing three crows is a sign that you're going to receive a letter while in other parts of the province three crows means a girl is going to come into your life in some profound way.

For Bonnie Keefe from Blockhouse, Nova Scotia, the number three accounts for the number of times she believes forerunners have come into her life, the first time being when she was about 15 years old and growing up in Cape Breton. She was visiting a cousin's home when the incident occurred.

"There were several of us there and we all saw it at the same time," Bonnie says. "We were just hanging out like teenagers do when we saw what looked like a person walking along the edge of the woods that bordered the property."

While Bonnie says they could not see the figure's face they all agreed that it was an older person and whoever it was, they were wearing an old-fashioned top hat.

"The strange part about the person is that they were all encompassed in white," she says. "We knew whoever or whatever it was, this was not a normal occurrence."

The teens later learned that at the same time that they had witnessed this figure surrounded in white, an older man from the area had passed away.

"I really don't think it was a coincidence," she says. "The more I've thought about it over the years the more convinced I am that what we saw that day was a forerunner of the old man who died. Beyond that, I'm not really sure what else it would have been."

While this would have been the first time Bonnie experienced such a phenomenon, she says it was not the last.

The hands of time

Years later, in 2001, after she had been married with a family of her own, Bonnie says she and her husband made the decision to relocate to Blockhouse on the province's South Shore where they had purchased a cottage. The cottage had a basement where she says the family kept a computer.

It was also where she and her husband kept memorabilia and family heirlooms on display including a pocket watch that her husband had inherited from his father.

"My husband was five years old when his father died so that watch hadn't been running for many years," she says. "In truth, we didn't even think the watch even worked."

Bonnie says it was the strangest thing but one evening while her daughter was on the computer down in the basement, the watch just started ticking. "It had been years since that watch was running," she says. "We had no idea what got it started but I took it as a sign."

There's an old saying that suggests when an old clock starts running for no apparent reason, it's a sign that time is running out for someone. In fact, Bonnie says, that was the case.

"It wasn't long after the watch started ticking that we received a phone call with the news that the father of my husband's best friend had died," says Bonnie. "We were all very close and I was convinced that the pocket watch had been a warning of the older man's impending death."

Even more unusual was when they later moved the watch from its place in the basement it abruptly stopped running and it hasn't worked since. It was very strange, Bonnie says, but she has no doubt that the timing of the watch starting to tick for no reason and the death of a family friend was no coincidence.

The birds send a message

The third time a forerunner played a role in their lives was in 2012 and Bonnie says the events revolved around her husband.

"My husband leaves for work very early every morning," she points out. "Most times he's on the road before the sun comes up."

On this particular day, she says, he called her after he arrived at work to tell her that when he got out of his truck he discovered that he had hit a baby barred owl during his commute and its tiny body was still stuck in the vehicle's grill.

"It bothered him that he had hit the owl and he hadn't seen it until he got to work that morning," she says. "It was just too small for him to even hear it hit the truck so it was easy to understand how something like that could happen."

For Bonnie, she explains that she immediately concluded that the dead owl was a sign because she had heard that owls can be seen as a sign of impending death and the fact that this baby owl was killed left her with a sense of dread and foreboding. She believed that someone close to them was going to die.

"We had a very close friend who was dying with cancer and he was not good," Bonnie explains. "When my husband called to tell me about the baby owl, I immediately thought of our friend."

It wasn't long after her husband's call that she received another call telling her that their friend had succumbed to the cancer and had died at around 6:40 that morning, which, Bonnie says would have been around the exact same time her husband was driving to work.

Was the dead baby owl a sign to Bonnie and her husband that their friend was going to die?

Of course, there is no way to know for certain if that's the case but Bonnie believes that's exactly what happened.

"No question," she insists. "There is no doubt about it. It's just too much of coincidence."

Every man must do two things alone; he must do his own believing and his own dying.

— Martin Luther

The Picture on The Wall

A picture is worth a thousand words, but if a framed picture falls from the wall for no apparent reason, it can mean that someone you know is going to die within three days. Taking it a step further, if the glass shatters upon hitting the floor it means someone you are very close to will die within three days.

For people like Barbara Denton who lives in her centuries-old family home located in Kentville, Nova Scotia, such warnings are not to be ignored.

Barbara's story takes place in August 1984 when she and her husband Gilbert — who had only been married for just over a year — moved into the family home to take care of her aging parents. As an only child, she felt it was her responsibility to take care of her parents and to help them navigate some serious health issues they were facing.

It was early in the morning of August 24 shortly after Gilbert had left for work and Barbara was enjoying her typical morning ritual which included sitting at the kitchen table having a cup of coffee before she tackled the list of chores and errands she had planned for the day. Her parents were both still resting in the upstairs bedroom and other than her mother and father there was no one else in the house. Even the cat, Ember, was asleep in the living room.

It was only around 7 o'clock, she recalls, but it was already hot and very humid, signs that it was going to be a beautiful summer day. Sitting at the table and listening to the local news on the radio, Barbara was relaxed and not thinking of anything in particular. It was her favourite time of day.

Crash, bang, shatter

About five minutes into her coffee, she was startled by a loud bang followed by the unmistakable sound of shattering glass. She jumped to her feet, and her first thought was that one of her parents had gotten out of bed and had fallen. She quickly ran up to the bedroom, and was relieved to find her mother was still sleeping while her father was up and in the bathroom.

No, he told her, he had not fallen. He also told her that he had not heard anything like a thud, so whatever she had heard it hadn't come from any place on the second floor.

Barbara says she thought that was very strange because she was certain something had broken. A wave of apprehension quickly washed over her body. She was sure that she had heard a smashing sound. Whatever it was, the incident left her feeling unsettled.

As a shroud of dread wrapped its cold arms tightly around her, she says she immediately felt a deep feeling of sadness. What could have caused the crash, she wondered?

After checking on her mother who was still resting comfortably in bed and scouting out the three bedrooms and bathroom on the upstairs level and finding everything in its place, Barbara moved to the first floor and began searching for the origin of the crashing sound.

Checking out the living room, she was shocked to discover that her parents' wedding picture that had been hanging on the wall behind the couch for as long as she could remember had fallen and the glass had completely shattered. This was very troubling.

"That picture had been hanging in that exact some spot for many years and it had never fallen before," says Barbara. "The only time it was ever taken down was for cleaning or if the walls were being painted."

Barbara knew it was a sign that someone she was very close to was going to die within three days. She became overwhelmed with the possibility of losing one of her family members and Barbara says the days that followed this event were among the darkest she has ever endured. No matter how hard she tried to push the shattered glass from her mind, the awful feeling of dread kept invading her thoughts.

In the late afternoon of the following day, the truth she was so dreading for the past day and half was finally revealed to Barbara. When she went into her parents' bedroom to awaken her mother from her nap, she discovered her mother passed into the next world.

Do not go gentle into that good night... Rage, rage against the dying of the light.

— Dylan Thomas

Something in the Air

In folklore, smells are not typically associated with forerunners, because they aren't as tangible as a visual apparition or as a sound. That does not mean, however, that a smell can't be considered a warning that tragedy is about to strike.

Tales of certain smells, such as the sweet scent of a woman's perfume, your mother's favourite flower, the smell of freshly baking bread wafting from the kitchen or grandpa's favourite tobacco pipe, have been associated with paranormal activity for many generations so we know odours can also sometimes be carrying a deeper meaning than we may have thought.

Leah and Jeff Rissesco, who live in a picturesque Smith's Cove in Lower Vaughn, Nova Scotia, can attest to the power of a smell because they experienced the phenomena first-hand.

Leah starts the story, remembering that the events happened many years earlier when their son James was very young.

"He was just about two years old at the time," she says, remembering that when she went to his room to get him after he woke up from his nap, she was alarmed that she could smell smoke — cigarette smoke.

"And that was more than weird because neither of us smoked," she quickly points out.

In fact, the smell was so strong that she called Jeff and he immediately came to check out the room.

"He looked around but he couldn't find anything," Leah recalls. "But we could both smell the smoke. It was very strong and pretty distinct."

The smoke smell hung in the air for ten or fifteen minutes before it was gone.

Export "A"

They received the answer to that question the following Sunday in church when they ran into the niece of the man who had owned the house before they purchased the property about five years earlier. His name was Ivan.

"We asked her how her uncle was doing, only to find out he had died a few days earlier," Jeff explains. Then it all clicked in, he adds.

"Her uncle had been a heavy smoker and his favourite brand of cigarettes was Export A," he points out.

They were able to put two and two together when they learned from the man's niece that the day her uncle died was the same day that Leah and Jeff smelled the smoke in their son's room.

It had been at least five years since Ivan had been in Leah and Jeff's house, but had the man returned to visit one last time before he died?

And when great souls die, after
a period peace blooms, slowly and
always irregularly. Spaces fill with a
kind of soothing electric vibration.
Our senses, restored, never to be the
same, whisper to us. They existed.
They existed. We can be. Be and be
better. For they existed.

— Maya Angelou

A Special Gift

Do some people have a special gift that allows them to talk with the deceased, see dead people or foretell the future? Can they sense when disaster is about to strike or when a loved one is about to die? Can they see a tragedy before it happens?

It has been established that some people do, indeed, possess such powers, a sixth sense if you will.

Pam Foley, who lives with her husband, Brian, in a rustic home in Milton, Nova Scotia, just outside of Liverpool, believes some members of her family have such abilities. You be the judge.

"My mom never believed in ghosts, but she did believe in forerunners, which were more acceptable to her because she believed they were authenticated by the events that followed."

Gala was born in 1935 and lived around the town of Liverpool her entire life and she passed along her belief in such superstitions to own children. Pam vividly recalls the stories she heard as a youngster as related by her mother.

"When she was a young girl, my mother remembers sitting with her family one evening when her father's hat just fell off a hook on the wall. At that time, he had been away, working in the woods. My grandmother looked up from her needlework and said to her family, 'Your father's just been hurt.' And sure enough, he arrived home the next day with a broken leg."

Coincidence? Maybe, but there's more.

"When my grandmother died in the hospital, my mother had two experiences that she believed confirmed the existence of forerunners. For one, she heard her name being called out even though there was no one else in the house. Secondly, at that very same moment, a bird flew into the house."

A foreshadowing

In the Maritimes, these signs are labeled as forerunners, tokens or omens. They are considered a foreshadowing of some tragic event about to occur, usually involving a family member or a close personal friend.

"Mom knew these signs were a bad omen," Pam says. It was only a short time later she received word that her mom had passed away."

And Pam has one more story about her mother's gift.

"In 1976, on a Sunday, my father, Allen Manthorne, suffered a stroke and was in hospital in Halifax recovering," she says. "My mother was taken to his sister's house in the city to stay there so she could be close to the hospital."

A few days later, they received word that her father had eaten a nice meal and was now resting comfortably. That was good news, as it appeared he was on the road to recovery.

"Everyone felt better at the news. Mom had gone to bed for the night, prepared to visit my dad in the hospital again the next morning," Pam recalls.

"When she was almost asleep, she suddenly opened her eyes to see a shadow enter her bedroom. It was the size of a man, but she told us it didn't have any particular form or features. It settled itself at the foot of mom's bed. She could feel the weight against her legs and it seemed to watch her for a while. Later that same night, the hospital phoned to say Dad had unexpectedly taken a turn for the worse and the family should go to him right away."

Allen was dead before his family could make it to the hospital. He was 42.

"Mom always believed that the visitor to her room that night was my father's way of trying to see her one more time before he died, and to let her know what was happening."

The gift

Pam believes her mother had the gift, and she recalls yet another story involving Gala's experience.

"Another time, in the early 1990s, Mom was travelling with her companion down some rather deserted hauling roads in the woods, in his truck, in January, in the bitter cold. The truck broke down and, realizing they might die if they remained there in the cold, her companion set out on foot to get help," she explains.

"Mom expected he'd be right back, so she stayed behind with the truck and waited for help to arrive. She waited and she waited a *long* time. Eventually though, she too set out on foot, thinking maybe her friend was in trouble. Fatigue and cold finally got to her, and she collapsed beneath a tree. As she sat there freezing, she started to feel warm and sleepy. Just as she was nodding off, a lady wearing a long black skirt arrived and kept her awake until eventually her friend arrived with help. Just as quickly as the mysterious woman appeared, she disappeared. Mom never saw a face, and she didn't have a clue about who the lady could have been, but she believed the woman saved her life."

Pam's mother died of cancer in 1993, but not before experiencing yet another unexplained phenomenon.

"One evening, near the end, she lay awake in pain, wishing for some relief," Pam explains. "She was thankful to feel someone crawl into bed with her and hold her in their arms through the night so she could get some sleep. She was living with my family at the time, and commented the next morning that she really needed that special touch through the night and thanked whoever it was that had come to comfort her. However, none of us had spent the night with her, but I always believed something special happened to Mom that night."

Did Gala have a guardian angel or was she just overly superstitious? It's hard to say, but it is clear through all of these experiences that she seemed to be tuned in to a realm outside of what most of us consider normal.

Perhaps these things can be explained, but sometimes it's better to suspend logic. Sometimes it's more enlightening just to suspend belief and accept things that have no simple explanation.

I think you should be serious about what you do because this is it. This is the only life you ve got.

— Philip Seymour Hoffman

What Did You Say?

L isa Roy from Yarmouth says she grew up hearing stories about forerunners. She says when her grandmother, aunts and mother were alive and all in the same room the stories would come fast and furious.

"Whenever they were together, they just loved to talk about this stuff," Lisa continues. "And honestly, I enjoy it too. Besides, it's fascinating to hear people tell their stories so I love to listen."

She says she especially likes hearing about the personal experiences and encounters that other members of her family have had over the years and adds that her grandmother, though, was the maser storyteller in the family.

"Yes, forerunner stories are sad because they always end with someone dying," says Lisa, "but I believe that there is some kind of force out there in the universe that allows someone to reach out to us to prepare us for what is about to happen. I just find the whole idea very comforting because it reaffirms there are things happening all around us that we can't explain."

A personal story

Lisa says she has also had her own personal encounters with fore-runners and in particular she recalls an experience back in 2018 in which her then deceased grandmother played a role.

"Grammie had died about 10 years earlier but I still missed her," she says. "She was a very special woman in my life and we were very close. She lived a good, long life so when her time was up we all had the feeling that she was ready to go. I never got the sense from her that she was afraid of dying or anything like that. In fact, she always told us that death was part of living and we had to accept that. She was very direct."

But even in death, Lisa says she still feels very close to her grandmother.

"I knew Grammie was gone and I would never see her again, but I still feel her presence all around me even to this day," she says. "Grammie helped me through some very tough times including the death of my own mother back in 2018."

Her mother had been suffering with cancer for a number of years so her death wasn't really unexpected, but it was still diffi-cult for Lisa to accept that she was gone.

"It was hard watching as she fought and suffered for those two years before she finally died but even though we all expected it, it's still a shock when it happens. I took her death very hard."

Lisa does take some comfort in knowing that her mother and grandmother are together now and she feels she knows that for certain because of an experience she had just days before her mother's death. She recalls the events of that hot August day very clearly.

"I had worked a long hard shift that day and it was particularly rough," she says. "Not only did everything seem to go wrong at work, but I was worried about mom. I knew she was in a bad way and I just couldn't shake the feeling that the end was very close. I couldn't stop thinking about her."

She recalls the first thing that she did when she got home was to plop on the couch and close her eyes.

"I just had to catch my breath. Maybe it was the heat or all the pressure at work or this thing mom was going through, but I felt like I was at my breaking point."

She no sooner hit the couch, laid her head on a pillow and closed her eyes, she says, before she dozed off.

"I was asleep for maybe fifteen minutes when I suddenly awoke to the sound of someone calling my name," Lisa says. "I recognized the voice right away. It was my grandmother reaching out to me to let me know that my mother was soon going to die. I knew Grammie came to get me ready for the inevitable and when the call finally came it really wasn't such a shock."

In fact, later that evening Lisa says one of her sisters called to tell her she should come to the hospital right away because their mother had taken a turn for the worse and she wasn't expected to make it through the night.

Her mother died early the next morning.

"It was hard," she says. "As you might expect, but the fact that my grandmother had prepared me for what was about to happen, made it a little easier to accept that my mother was gone."

While she is certain about what she heard that afternoon, Lisa admits that she knows some people find it hard to accept that her grandmother had come to her to prepare her for the bad news and she accepts their opinions.

"But I know what I heard that day and it was her. She said 'Lisa.' There was a short pause. 'Lisa.' There was another short pause and then she said 'Lisa' again and then I woke up. It wasn't a dream and it was my emotions. It was a clear as any conversation I've ever had. No one else has to believe it, but I do."

I hope the exit is joyful and hope never to return.

— Frida Kahlo

The Light and the Darkness

Some people seem more connected to the spiritual world than others and some people like Dianne Wamboldt of Milton, Nova Scotia will insist that when you encounter something as unusual as a forerunner you tend to accept that you've just experienced something beyond the normal world as we know it.

Or at least that's what Dianne chose to do, not once but twice.

In fact, the first incident happened almost 50 years ago but even after all of this time she still remembers the events as if they occurred yesterday.

She was 32 weeks pregnant with her only child so that may account for some of her sharp recall. She remembers being confined to bed rest on doctor's orders as she was experiencing some complications with the pregnancy. Dianne recalls the events took place on a Sunday evening.

"I was resting in bed and David (her husband) was out in the living room. I was just lying there, not thinking about anything in particular, when I watched as a white-smoky cloud-like form entered the bedroom, hover for a few seconds, and then just float right on through the room."

Dianne could not make out any distinguishable features like a face or anything like that, but she knew in the pit of her stomach that it had been something out of the ordinary.

"It just felt like it was something unusual had just happened but when I told David about it he dismissed what I had seen," she remembers. "What he told me I had seen were the lights of a passing vehicle from the nearby road, but I told him I knew that I had seen a forerunner."

She accepts that not everyone pleases in such things.

"He didn't believe me and I didn't really expect that he would, but I was worried because David's grandfather was really sick at the time and we were expecting to get a call anytime that he had died," Dianne says. "I knew all about forerunners because I had heard about them growing up and I believed that a forerunner had come to me to tell me about David's grandfather."

But that wasn't it all, she points out.

An unexpected call

Death did follow, however. Less than a week after Dianne had seen the cloudy-white formation in her bedroom, she received an unexpected call that her 58-year-old mother had suddenly died without warning.

"We were shocked because my mother wasn't sick at the time," Dianne says. "The doctors told us it was a massive heart attack and that's when I knew that what I had seen that night was mom's forerunner."

Even today, after all of these years, Dianne is still convinced that what she saw that Sunday evening was a harbinger of her mother's death.

And again

A second incident that occurred over the holiday season years later only confirmed for Dianne what she says she had known for years — that forerunners are real and should not be readily dismissed.

She and David had been attending a Christmas party at a friend's home located about a ten-minute drive from their own house.

The hour was late, Dianne remembers. She drove the car home from the party and she says it was an especially dreary night — foggy and pitch black. "It was the kind of night that made driving especially difficult so you had to be really careful and pay close attention to the road."

Dianne was doing fine on the drive home and everything seemed normal up to the point where the road in front of her made a slight curve and then immediately took a little dip. That's when she saw it.

"As I came around the bend and went into this little dip, all of sudden I saw this body laying right in the middle of the road," Dianne says.

She slammed on the brakes, coming to an abrupt stop dead in

the road with David immediately asking her what she was happening. Was something wrong, he asked her?

Something in the road

"Yes," she told him. "There's someone laying in the road."

"Where?" David asked. He didn't see anything, but she did.

"I put the high-beam lights on and slowly inched the car forward," Dianne says. "But as I got closer to whoever that was laying in the middle of the road, the image just disappeared. David said I was seeing things in the dark and fog, but I knew what I had seen and there was definitely someone there."

The following weekend after her encounter with the body in the road, Dianne tells the story of family relatives who were travelling on the same road that she and David had taken. These relatives too had been attending a social function on that evening, and the husband in the couple had been complaining throughout the evening that he had not been feeling well so his wife was driving home.

At some point during the drive he asked his wife if she would pull the car over so that he could get out as he wanted to walk the rest of the way home. It wasn't far but he felt that the fresh air and exercise would do him good and hopefully make him feel better. He told his wife to go home and he would see her shortly.

So, thinking that her husband might be right about the walk and seeing that it was only a short distance to the house, she let him out of the car and drove away.

When her husband failed to show up by the allotted time she had estimated it would take for him to walk there, she asked her son to go look for his father and to make sure he was all right.

While taking the same route his mother had travelled only minutes earlier, the son subsequently discovered his father sprawled in the middle of the road. He was dead. Doctors later determined the man had suffered a massive heart attack and died instantly.

The man's body was discovered in the exact same location in the road where Dianne had seen the body laying only a week earlier.

Was this all a coincidence?

No, Dianne insists. Not at all. She is absolutely positive that what she had seen that night on the road was the man's forerunner.

"I am absolutely positive," she says without hesitation. "I have no doubt in mind that it was a forerunner. ... What else would it have been?"

What else, indeed?

I'm about to take my last voyage, a great leap into the dark.

— Thomas Hobbes

The Woman in the Cemetery

Katherine MacIntosh says that while she grew up in a household very much immersed in the in the spiritual world, she didn't fall into the same category. She had always remained sceptical of things that defied explanation because for her there was always an explanation for the "unexplained."

You just had to look for it.

That was before the events of June 10, 2019, when this Cape Breton-born and raised mother of three says she had an experience that she has never been able to explain or forget.

June 10, 2019, was an unusually overcast and dreary day with dense fog and heavy mist. It was the kind of day that created an ominous feeling. Katherine remembers just being jumpy and on edge the whole time.

"Basically, I felt terrible for the entire day," she says. From the moment that I got up that morning, I just couldn't shake it and it basically left me feeling physically drained and incapable of thinking or doing anything constructive."

She now believes there was a logical explanation for how she was feeling. That was the day she received a warning about her maternal grandmother. Growing up, there was no one closer to Katherine than her grandmother Victoria and that continued into adulthood.

A special bond

"I just worshiped the ground that woman walked on," says Katherine. "Grammie and I just seemed to have this special bond. Sure, she loved all of her grandchildren but she always told me I was special and she always made feel special. Maybe it was because I was the youngest grandchild."

Katherine recalls spending many hours with her grandmother learning how to cook and bake, and how to knit. "Grammie taught me so much that I attribute to who I am today to what I learned from her. We were inseparable and I could never think of my world without having her in it."

But, as Katherine learned, life does happen and she learned that lesson the hard way in June 2019. She remembers the events as if they occurred just yesterday because, as she says, "They are seared into my brain. I don't think that I will never forget them."

In fact, she quickly points out, on June 10, 2019, she says she came to believe that there are some things that cannot easily be explained.

Visiting dad

Katherine's father had died 20 years earlier following a lengthy battle with cancer when she was only 15. She loved him deeply and missed him profoundly. It upsets her to think that he missed her graduation, her wedding day and the birth of her three children but she eventually came to terms with her loss. Often times, when she felt sad, she felt the urge to visit her father's grave.

"I can't explain it but visiting dad's grave always made me feel better. It's like we connected, somehow," she says.

On June 10, 2019, she left her children with her husband and drove to the cemetery. She talked to her father like she always did. This evening though things were different. She had no sooner finished her visit at her father's grave when she saw what she now believes was a forerunner. There was a woman in black.

"I was shocked," Katherine says while pointing out that as far as she knew, she was alone in the cemetery that evening so she wasn't expecting to see anyone there. "And I admit that I immediately felt scared because I thought I was alone and I didn't know what I was seeing."

Now keep in mind, it was still extremely foggy so while many people will argue that her eyes were probably playing tricks on her because of the weather conditions, she is 100 per cent certain that what she saw that evening was, indeed, the real thing — a forerunner.

A woman in black

"Based on its size and stature, I could tell it was a woman, but not a young woman, an older woman, someone I would describe as kind of feeble and weak. She was bent over and I could make out physical features, but I couldn't see her face because she held her head down and the fog was thick."

"I saw her walk through the front gates of the cemetery and then turn to head in the direction where I was standing. One minute she was walking toward me and then the next minute she was suddenly gone."

It all happened very quickly, Katherine says, and she froze in her tracks.

"I mean, I literally could not move. It was like my feet where stuck to the ground and they refused to listen to my brain that was telling me to get out of there."

But she couldn't budge so she just stood there, watching as the figure in black moved toward her.

"I got goosebumps and shook, but I can't really say I was scared or anything like that. It's just that I was shocked because I knew in my heart of hearts that this 'woman' was a forerunner and as I stood there watching 'her' come towards to me, all I could think about were those stories that I had heard over the years about people seeing these strange things and what it really meant according to superstitions."

Forerunner

Katherine understood the forerunner was warning her that someone close to her was soon going to die and that death would occur within the next three days.

The death that followed was unexpected because for the most part, despite her age, Katherine believed her beloved 86-year-old grandmother was in good health, but two days after the incident in the cemetery, the elderly woman passed without warning.

"The doctor said she died peacefully in her sleep so we take some comfort in knowing that she did not suffer. They said it was a major stroke and she likely never woke up."

Holding back her tears, she continues, "But it was still hard to accept that Grammie was gone. I miss her so much even after all these years. There's just a big, empty hole in my heart that I don't think will ever heal."

As to what she saw that foggy evening in the cemetery, Katherine believes, without question, the elderly woman she encountered was not her grandmother but rather a messenger sent to her as a warning that a major life-changing event was about to take place and that she should prepare for something tragic to happen.

"So, when you ask me if I believe in forerunners, the answer is simple — yes I do. They are real ... as real as you and me; it's just that they aren't anything you can easily explain."

Now, she says, when someone tells her they experienced a forerunner she believes them.

"I was one of those people who shrugged her shoulders and dismissed the stories as just 'crazy talk' but not anymore."

Applaud, my friends, the comedy
is finished.

— Ludwig Van Beethoven

Knocks and Moths and Shadows

There are some people who say they have believed in fore-runners their entire life. They will, without hesitation, admit that having paranormal experiences has become such a regular occurrence in their lives that they simply accept when it happens without question while at the same time bracing for the subsequent bad news that's sure to follow.

This is Claudine Bulley who was raised in Liverpool, the historical privateering port on Nova Scotia's South Shore. A community steeped in folklore and superstition where tales of the unusual and supernatural are fairly common, forerunner stories are part of the local fabric. She says it was only natural then that some of her beliefs were influenced by her home community.

"There was no getting away from stories of the supernatural world when I was growing up," she says. "There were stories about seeing strange things and having strange experiences, but I was never scared because of those stories."

Sooner or later Claudine says she started having experiences involving forerunners and each time she received one she knew what would follow.

One of the experiences that stands out for Claudine was the time a few years ago when she heard several loud knocks from somewhere in the house. While she wasn't exactly sure where the sound originated, she believed she knew what it meant.

Sure enough, several days later she received word that her biological grandfather had passed away despite being in relatively good health.

Dark signs

Years later she received a sign that preceded the sudden death of a close friend.

"It was the strangest thing," she recalls. "I wasn't thinking about anything like this, but I simply watched as a large, black moth — probably the largest moth I had ever seen in my life — as it flew into my room and flitted all around the room for about a minute then it just disappeared."

Sure enough, several days later, she received word that a close family friend had died suddenly in his sleep of a major heart attack.

"That one left me shaken," she admits. "Not the appearance of the moth, but the death of my friend." In fact, she had already accepted that the black moth had been a forerunner and that a death would soon follow.

"I've experienced enough things over the years to know that's how it works."

A more recent encounter with her third forerunner only solidified her beliefs. As before, this experience started with several knocks, only in this incident the sound clearly originated at the front door.

Somebody's knocking

Going to see who was knocking Claudine says she was surprised that when she opened the door there was no one there.

"I was absolutely certain that I heard someone knocking at the front door," she insists. As Claudine closed the front door and turned around to return to the kitchen, she was startled to see an image of a man standing in the kitchen doorway.

"It scared the bejesus out of me," she says. "I was alone in the house at the time but there he was standing in front of me wearing a black overcoat.

"I could not see his face so I have no idea who it was but I could tell for certain that it was a man," Claudine explains. "And he just stood there for maybe a minute or so and then he just disappeared. To this day I have no idea for certain who it was."

But, she adds, she has her suspicions.

"I believe what I saw in the doorway of my kitchen was the forerunner of a man from our neighbourhood who I later heard had died that day," she says. "Although I'm not really certain why he would come to me about his impending death because we really weren't that close, I am sure it was him."

Like all things connected with the paranormal, the definite answer to that question remains a mystery. However, she says, that point does not change the fact that she is certain of what she experienced that day and she is absolutely positive that she saw a forerunner, just as she had throughout her entire life.

"I know some people don't believe in such things," she says. "But I do. I know forerunners are real because I've had too many experiences not to believe."

We are all in the gutter, but some of us are looking at the stars.

— Oscar Wilde

There and Gone

True friendship can withstand many tests — the passage of time, great geographical distances, social challenges and even an impending death.

Such was the case for Silvana Redden of Middle Musquodoboit, Nova Scotia, and her childhood friend Andy who had moved to Toronto many years before the events of this story took place.

Growing up in the picturesque seaport of Digby on Nova Scotia's French Shore, Silvana and Andy formed a life-long friendship, a bond that persisted even as they grew into adults and followed their life paths, she with her own family of four children, ten grandchildren and four great-grandchildren, and he teaching in Toronto.

The two kept in touch for a while but in time they drifted apart. No matter how much time passed, however, or how much distance separated them, she always considered Andy to be a special friend from her childhood.

"We just clicked as kids, but when life pulls you in separate directions sometimes you just can't find the time to keep in close contact," Silvana says. "But even if you don't often see them, you always keep a special place in your heart and memories for those special types of friends."

So that's how it was with Andy, a special friend who played a special role in Silvana's life.

"I knew my grandmother had this uncanny ability to know things before they happened," she says, recalling an event when she was just an eleven-year-old child still living in Digby.

"It was just the strangest thing. My grandmother actually called the house one afternoon to see how I was doing or if I was hurt because she said she believed I had fallen off of my bike. I had not but sure enough later that day, I fell riding my bike."

Embrace the experience

It was these strange little "happenings" that confirmed for Silvana that her grandmother was special, so years later when she had her own experiences she embraced them.

"When these things happen to me or when I hear other people talking about things that have happened to them, I never dismiss them," Silvana says. "I've learned long ago just to accept that when these things happen, they can't always be easily explained and because I know they always happen for a reason."

It had been years since she had seen Andy or even spoken with him for that matter, but Silvana says when she looked up one evening and saw him standing in her living room looking down at her she immediately knew what she was seeing.

"I knew right away it was a forerunner," she says. "And I immediately recognized Andy even though at that point in my life I hadn't seen him in many years. I just knew it was him and I knew this was a sign that he was going to die."

While she admits that seeing her life-long friend out of the blue like that was a shock for her, she also says without hesitation that she was not afraid.

"He was only there for maybe a minute — if that long — and then, just like that, he was gone," she explains. "I knew he didn't come to frighten me but instead he had come to say his goodbyes. I knew this would be the last time I would ever see Andy so it made me sad not scared."

Experiencing such a phenomenon can often be an unsettling experience for many people, but Silvana says it gave her comfort to understand that her good friend had actually reached out to her in his diminishing time here on earth.

"I still think of Andy, often, and I am grateful that he reached out to me when his end was near," she says, adding that this experience confirmed something she had already known for a very long time — that forerunners are real.

Death is the dropping of the flower
that the fruit may swell.

— Henry Ward Beecher

The Song of the Whip-poor-will

Bill Williams was born and raised in Nova Scotia and tells of his experience around the death of his sick father, Raymond. We pick up the story in August 2016.

Bill's father had been sick for almost a year and confined to hospital with liver cancer. "It was a terrible time for everyone in the family because Dad was in excruciating pain. No one wanted to see him die but it was hard seeing him like that. I couldn't stand to watch him suffer, but there was nothing they could do for him except keep him comfortable."

Bill had always been close to his father. They enjoyed many hours traipsing all over Nova Scotia looking for birds.

"Dad was an avid birdwatcher and I remember him packing us up and heading off to different places to look for various rare species that he needed to add to his list," Bill explains.

"He kept extensive and detailed records of every bird he had seen over the years including the date, time and location. He would also include details about how many were in a flock or if it was a solitary bird."

Trips with dad

"I really enjoyed those trips with dad," Bill recalls. "We spent many hours together out and about in the wilderness and remote areas of Nova Scotia. We would travel from one end of the province to the other. Those trips became our special time and when I think of those time, I'm happy to have the memories."

As Bill grew older and his interests took him elsewhere, his adventures with his father soon became fewer and fewer until eventually, they stopped altogether. But he knew his father continued to search for rare and elusive birds, all the while keeping extensive records of his journeys.

"I'm very glad to say I have all of my father's record books," Bill says. "They're kind of my way of keeping him close to me."

One of the things he recalls about his father was his uncanny talent to mimic the birdcalls.

Over the years, his father had perfected dozens of birdcalls but the one that he loved the most was doing the song of the whip-poor-will, a medium-sized nightjar found throughout North America. The whip-poor-will is commonly heard within its range, but is very difficult to spot because of its camouflage, which allows it to practically hide in plain sight. It is named onomato-

"The way Dad could mimic that bird was simply beautiful," Bill proudly proclaims. "It was mesmerizing the way he could make that bird come to life by duplicating its song. He entertained many people with his skills."

A unique talent

It was Raymond's unique talent to duplicate the song of the whip-poor-will that united father and son as death was approaching.

"I spent as much time as I could in the hospital with Dad. Thank God, I run my own business because that gave me the flexibility to come and go, as I needed. During the last few weeks of Dad's life, I was at the hospital more than I was at the office or at home, for that matter, but I just had to be there with him. Mom had died a few years earlier and my sisters live out of the province, so it was just me and I couldn't leave him alone."

They were difficult weeks, Bill remembers, as the emotions on his face betray the raw pain that he continues to suffer to this day.

Near the end, Bill says he could tell that his father was slipping away and it took all his strength to sit beside the bed and watch the man that he loved fade from this world into whatever waited on the other side.

"I remember it was late in the afternoon on a Thursday in August when the nurse who was keeping watch over him came to me and told me I should go home for bit just to give myself a break. She could tell I was nearing the end of my rope. I was exhausted and emotionally drained. She suggested that an hour or so away from the hospital would do me good and she promised that if anything changed, she would call me right away so that I could come back and be with Dad."

Even though Bill felt guilty about leaving his father's side, he thought that maybe a brief reprieve might actually do him good so he agreed to go home but only after the nurse assured him that she would call at even at the slightest of changes in his father's condition.

"Since I only live about 10 minutes from the hospital it meant I could get back quickly if Dad needed me, I went home where I found the house was empty. My wife was at work and our children were spending time with their friends so the place was quiet."

Reaching out

Stopping at the kitchen counter to check the mail that had been piled there, Bill says he had just begun to make his way through the letters when, out of the blue, he heard a whip-poor-will.

"It stopped me cold in my tracks," says Bill. "I froze. I mean, I literally could not move. The chills ran up my back and the little hairs on my arms rose as I shook from head to toe. I had heard that bird call too many times not to recognize it for what it was. I knew, without a doubt, that it was a whip-poor-will."

But how could that be? There was no one else in the house except Bill. All the radios and televisions were off. There was simply no explanation for what he had heard.

No worldly explanation, that is.

"I was dumbfounded, really. I honestly didn't know what to do and for a few seconds, I just stood there wondering what to do next. I thought my mind must be playing tricks on me because there was simply no way I could have heard what I thought I had heard."

Then he heard the song again, for a second time.

"And this time, I knew right away what was going on," Bill says, choking back tears. "I knew it was the whip-poor-will and I knew it was Dad."

Immediately after the second birdcall, his cell phone rang and he knew what was coming.

"I knew that Dad had died before I answered the phone," Bill says. "I am convinced that Dad knew he was going to die and he waited until I left the room to do it because he didn't want me to be there when it happened. I honestly believe that he didn't want me to see him die because he thought it would be too painful for me to witness."

As to the song of the whip-poor-will, Bill says he knows what he heard that day in his house and he is 100 per cent certain that it was the birdcall that his father used to make.

"I believe in my heart that Dad reached out me as he was dying and sent that whip-poor-will song to me as a message," he says. "I am sure that Dad was telling me that I should not worry about him because he was going to be alright and that he was no longer in any pain."

Call it a forerunner or whatever you want, but for Bill that song of the whip-poor-will was the last thing he ever received from his father and he takes comfort in the fact that while he can't logically explain what happened to him that day, he is certain that his father is doing okay and is no longer suffering.

The taste of death is upon my lips. I feel something that is not of this earth.

— Mozart

Messengers of Death

I have always been a believer in such things, even as a child," says Brenda King from Lockeport, the small coastal village located in Shelburne County.

The mother of three and grandmother of seven says, "It really wasn't anything that I ever really thought about all that much. It's just that I always believed there were things out there that I couldn't explain or understand."

After two personal experiences with forerunners, she is more certain than ever that such things do exist. "You don't have to understand something for it to be real," she says.

Her first experience occurred in 2020 and involved an

encounter with her grandmother.

"Now, you should know that I never really knew my grandmother on my mother's side of the family," Brenda explains, pointing out that her grandmother had passed away before she was born. "I had seen pictures of her so I knew what she looked like and I had heard descriptions of her general features so I had a pretty good idea of how she would have appeared."

It was that knowledge that convinced Brenda that she had encountered her grandmother just a short while before her own mother passed away.

"I am positive it was the older woman and she came to warn me that I should be prepared for tragedy. I knew it was a forerunner but I had no idea that it would be a warning about my mother."

Just an ordinary day

Describing the experience, Brenda remembers that the day wasn't anything exceptional, just a normal day at the Lockeport Nursing Home where she had worked for 30 years.

Late in the afternoon, however, her day turned upside down. She wasn't thinking about anyone is particular, just doing tasks around the house that needed to be done, then all of sudden there "she" was.

"Just as plain as if I can see her now, there was my grandmother standing there in the doorway," Brenda says. "I just knew it was her."

She says the image of the woman remained in the doorway for a few minutes and then vanished just as quickly as she had appeared, leaving Brenda to make sense out of what she had just witnessed.

And while Brenda points out that she wasn't afraid of what she had just seen, she admits the experience had left her emotionally drained and overwhelmed, and she could not shake the oppressive feeling of dread that swept over her.

"I knew the stories about forerunners so I believed this vision had been a warning to me," Brenda says.

In short order Brenda heard that her mother had died unexpectedly.

"It all came together and made sense to me. I was devastated that my mother was gone but I took comfort in the fact that my grandmother had reached out to me and I honestly believe she was trying to tell me not to worry, that everything was going to be all right."

Her second encounter with a forerunner — well, actually, it was her first — came in 2013 and involved her ailing husband, Rickie. She explains her husband, a former military man, had been ill for quite some time so she wasn't surprised when they began to experience strange visions in their house. However, while she could sense something was going on at that time, she explains it was Rickie who actually saw the forerunner.

"And he saw it several times," she adds.

The first visit

Pointing out she remembers the events of that time very well, she says she was in another part of the house when she heard Rickie calling for her to come and help him. When she got to the room where her husband had been resting she found him upset and distraught.

"He kept asking me if had seen her," Brenda says. "I kept asking 'had I seen who?'"

Once she settled him she says Rickie asked her if she had seen his aunt. He had seen her outside the house and he insisted that he saw her through the window.

She admits the question caught her off guard because once he described what he had seen, Brenda too believed that he had seen his aunt. The only catch was that Rickie's aunt had been dead for several years..

"But he insisted he had seen her that day… and several more times after that."

Brenda says she had no idea what to do with that information but she refused to dismiss Rickie's feelings off-hand without considering all the options.

"I believed it could have something more," she says. "And, as it turned out, it certainly was."

Two days after her husband had seen his aunt walk past the window for the first time, he died.

"I absolutely believe that Rickie saw a forerunner," she insists. "He was so upset when he saw it … I believe it."

And the truth is, forerunners often come with a tremendous burden of dread and foreboding. That's understandable considering their reason for being present in the first place — to herald the arrival of death.

No one here gets out alive.

— Jim Morrison

Be Wary of Three Knocks at Night

Remember the old saying, "Be wary of things that go bump in the night?"

Well, for one Nova Scotian woman, those nighttime noises eventually led to a major loss in her family and now she has a warning for others — don't be so quick to dismiss things you don't understand or can't easily explain.

Wanda Lee Wentzell Baron of Mill Village, Queens County, remembers how agitated and upset her mother became one Christmas when, for no explanation, the family's Christmas tree lit up without anyone switching on the lights.

"I remember thinking at the time that it was very strange

because no one turned on the lights or anything but the tree just lit up," she says. "That type of thing happens for a reason."

It was a sign

Wanda Lee says her mother insisted that it was a sign that something bad was going to happen and just one day following the tree lighting incident her mother's father died suddenly.

"What else can you conclude other than the fact that the lit tree was a warning to the family telling them to be ready because someone close to them was soon going to die?" she says, pointing out that's how forerunners work.

"You experience these things without warning and then, bang, someone close to you suddenly dies." There is more than just this story, however, she says.

Several years ago she and her husband, John, shared an experience that reaffirmed her beliefs.

It was late at night in March of 1997 when, she recalls she and her husband were in bed sleeping when they were suddenly stirred awake by banging on the back door. They both heard it.

"There were three very loud and distinct knocks," she says.

Getting up to investigate who was at the door her first thought was that it must be her mom or dad because her parents lived across the road from them at the time. Given the late hour, she feared something must be wrong; perhaps someone was sick. When she got to the door though there was no one there.

It was very disturbing and Wanda Lee says she immediately felt her anxiety levels rise. "I knew right away this was a sign and I was scared because I understood that it meant someone close to me was going to die."

The following day was very difficult for her, she admits, explaining that she could not shake the feeling that something terrible was about to happen.

"I just felt this constant fear," she says. "I couldn't shake this nagging feeling all day long that I was going to receive word that somebody was hurt or had died. My husband was a carpenter and they worked outside a lot so I worried if something was going to happen to him."

The day passed without incident, and Wanda Lee thought perhaps she was off the hook. That night, however, after she and John had gone to bed, the pounding started again. "We both heard it, clear as day." Yet again, however, when they answered the door, no one was there.

Three more knocks

Getting up to investigate she says they were startled but not surprised.

"Honestly, this time, I was not expecting to find anyone when I opened the door," she says. "I've been around these things all my life and I just knew in my gut that I wouldn't see anyone."

And to make matters worse, Wanda Lee says there had been a light dusting of snow that evening so she became even more alarmed when she saw there were no footprints on the ground. "It's not a good feeling to understand that something is trying to warn you of an impending tragedy, but I just knew it was going to be something major."

On March 31, 1997, two days after Wanda Lee and John heard the second round of knocking on the front door, her mother called in the afternoon and told her she had to come over to their house right away because something was wrong with her father.

"I went right over," she recalls. "And when I got there, I found my father laying on the floor. He was unresponsive and he was hardly breathing."

Wanda Lee tried to perform CPR, but her father died.

"That's when I knew," Wanda Lee says, recalling those events as vividly as if they had just happened. "That's when I knew that the knocking on our front and back doors had been warnings."

She would later discover that three days prior to her own personal experiences, her brother Kevin had also heard three knocks at his home that he could not explain.

"That was just more proof that forerunners were at work in the days leading up to my father's death," she says "Not that I ever had any doubt, but when I heard about my brother's experience, it was just further confirmation that forerunners are real."

Remembering that you are going to die is the best way I know to avoid the trap of thinking you have something to lose.

— Steve Jobs

The Passenger in the Backseat

The long trek from Cape Breton to Halifax can be an arduous one.

If you're alone in your vehicle, especially if it's late at night it can also be nerve- wracking. And if you think you're alone in your car but it turns out you're not, it can be even more stressful..

John Baker originally hails from Cape Breton but he now lives and works in Halifax. One night in the summer of 2015 he had an experience that forever changed his perspective on life.

Halifax was in the grips of an extended heat wave that August and John's experience began as he was travelling back to Halifax. He had done the drive many times before, but this time, just an hour outside of Halifax he began feeling so sleepy that he felt he should pull over — just to be safe.

"I've spent thousands of hours on the road, and I don't ever remember when I've had to pull over and sleep," he says. "I was just drained and I assumed it must have been the heat."

On this particular night, he just felt he shouldn't push his luck.

"I tried everything I could think of to keep awake. I drank lots of coffee. I played the radio loud and I had the window rolled down to get lots of fresh air, but nothing was working," he remembers. "I was just too tired, and I could feel myself dozing off. I knew I had to get some sleep or I might have an accident."

Finding a wide section of open, straight highway, John pulled his car over onto the shoulder of the road, turned off the ignition, and closed his eyes. He dozed off immediately, but he wasn't asleep any more than maybe 10 or 15 minutes when he says he heard a man's voice.

Dreaming

"I wasn't dreaming. I know what I heard, and I am positive that I heard a voice in my car that night. The deep voice was that of a man, and it was simply repeating my name. 'John,' it said. Then there was a short pause. 'John,' it said again and then again. I heard it three times."

John remembers looking in his rearview mirror and catching a fleeting glimpse of a man in the backseat of his car.

"It was quick. He was there and then in an instant he was gone, but he was there long enough for me to get a good look at him and to know he was there, and I can tell you that I will never forget him."

It wasn't his imagination, he insists, describing the passenger in the backseat as middle-aged, maybe around 50, with black hair and a heavyset build, wearing a dark-coloured shirt.

Jumping from the car, John quickly opened all four doors and inspected the vehicle. He thought someone might have gotten in the car somehow while he was asleep.

"Now, you might say my mind was playing tricks on me. I know I was pretty tired, but I swear there was a strange man in the backseat of my car one minute, and then he was gone the next," he says. "I can't explain it but I'll admit that it left me pretty rattled. It was the strangest thing that ever happened to me."

Once John was sure there was no one else in the car, he gathered himself, turned on the ignition and resumed his trek back to Halifax, now fully awake.

"My heart was beating so fast in my chest and the adrenalin was flowing so quickly through my veins that I knew there was no longer any chance of me falling asleep again," he says.

Just over an hour later, he made it home.

Something unusual

The next day, during his lunch break, John was relaying his unusual experience to several of his co-workers. In turn, they kidded him, telling him that he was so exhausted from a week of partying his mind was just playing tricks on him.

But not everyone who heard his story was so quick to discount the tale. One of his colleagues, a middle-aged woman, asked if he believed in forerunners.

At first, he told her no, he didn't.

"She couldn't understand why I didn't believe in forerunners," he recalls. "As someone who had also grown up in Cape Breton, she was surprised by my confession because she believed everyone who grew up on the island believed in such things."

That, however was about to change because when John got home later that same day, his mother phoned him from Cape Breton with some devastating news.

"'John,'" she said, "and I could hear the trembling in her voice and could tell that she had been crying, 'You have to come right home because your father just died about an hour ago.'"

He admits that was the most difficult phone call he has ever received.

"I don't think there is any way you could ever be prepared for a phone call like that," John says, admitting that in hindsight he has always wondered if his co-worker had been right and that maybe he had seen a forerunner that night in his car.

"I don't know if it was a forerunner," he says, "but it was certainly a strange experience, I will tell you that much and I never want to experience anything like that ever again."

"

Life is for the living. Death is for the dead. Let life be like music. And death a note unsaid.

— Langston Hughes

It's a Mother and Daughter Thing

I have had too many experiences over the years to not believe," says Donna Lee Martin from Hunts Point, Queens County, adding without hesitation that she absolutely believes in fore-runners.

"For starters, my husband, Lloyd, saw my mother, who died in 1998, holding my son. The thing is, my son was born in 1999 and Lloyd saw my mother standing at my bedside on the first night we brought our son home from the hospital."

Sounds strange, she knows but Donna says Lloyd described the dress her mother was wearing when he saw her beside her daughter and it was the same one she was buried in. Lloyd would not have known that, she points out, because he didn't see her mother in her coffin.

"We have had many encounters with ghosts or spirits or whatever you choose to call them so I'm never surprised by anything like this. We regularly have 'visitors' in our house that make themselves known to us and it has been that way for many years."

Donna says her family is so used to them now that they have accepted the visitors as just a part of the house although she admits that they have all had times when they have felt uncomfortable in the house, especially if "they" are being really loud for some reason or they won't leave the doors closed.

"Those times we have had to go for drives, go outside for a while, yell at them to leave the door closed, just to get away for a little bit. Most of the time, though, they are just a part of our home and we have come to accept they are there," she says.

"I always tell my kids, the spirits are watching over us and are not there to hurt us. If they were going to hurt us, they would have done so years ago. I always feel they are there to protect us."

A mother's influence

Donna explains that her beliefs were inspired by her mother, who also believed in such extraordinary happenings.

"My mother had many experiences with forerunners," she explains. "A lot of times, she would have a forerunner and then shortly after she would get a call about a family member passing away. She was from a very large family and most of her relatives lived in Cape Breton while we lived in Liverpool. She always said, 'You never have to fear the dead; only the living will hurt you,' and that has always been a saying I agree with."

She points out that she has had many experiences in her own life that are of a "ghostly or supernatural" type.

"I once had a reading done before I had children and the psychic said I would have a child who would be very spiritual," Donna explains. "After I had my children, I discovered one of my sons could see spirits and ghosts. Right from when he just started talking, he would always ask us who the little boy on the stairs was."

We never saw the little boy ourselves for the first few years, but I have now seen him a few times. I accidentally saw him for the first time when he walked behind me one day in the kitchen and I followed him to the stairs and called after him, thinking it was my youngest son who has dark hair and dark eyes, the same as the young boy."

Her kids were quick to point out that they were both in the living room and she was calling to the little boy on the stairs, not her son.

Donna admits she isn't surprised when she has these types of encounters with spiritual beings because she experienced forerunners many times with her mom when she was younger.

Who's there?

"One of the first ones I remember happening directly to me was when my mother was dying at Queens General Hospital in August of 1998," she says. "My sister Karen and I were in her hospital room with her while my brother Kenny and sisters Debbie and Diane had gone to Chandlers to start the funeral arrangements. We had all been staying with her all week in the hospital."

Suddenly, she says, there was a loud knock on the hospital door.

"When I went out to see who it was, there was no one there or anywhere else in the hall. I made note of the time as I always do when something weird happens and when my siblings got back from Chandlers, my sister Diane commented that someone had tapped her on the shoulder at the funeral home and it was at the exact same time as I heard the knock."

Donna's mother died not too long after those incidents.

Another recent forerunner experience involved the family pet.

"My dog and I were lying in bed one night and there was a knock on the bedroom wall directly by my bed. I checked the time and hoped I wouldn't get any calls," Donna explains.

"A few days later I took my dog to the vet for a routine check-up for her eyes and ears and they discovered she had a mass in her throat and jaw area that they could do nothing for. She lasted only six weeks and then we lost her."

Donna is convinced the knocking on the wall was a warning about the dog's sickness and ultimate death.

Accurate predictions

Donna admits to sometimes being afraid when these things happen but only because she has seen forerunner predictions come true too many times in the past and when they happen, the first thing she always does is check the time.

"I then anxiously wait for a few days to see if I get any calls about losing a loved one. I sometimes get an uneasy feeling or a sense of doom and that always makes me very nervous as well because I always get a sense when something bad is happening or about to happen. Sometimes it turns out to be a feeling of dread and nothing amounts to it but I have had enough experiences of my own and with my Mom to always respect the forerunner and pray that things will be okay."

Donna says she believe in forerunners, ghosts, spirits and all things that some people can't or won't understand.

"Absolutely, 100 percent. I think my Mom being from Cape Breton had made a huge impact on my beliefs as a lot of people from there are very spiritual and connected to other worldly things."

She adds that if people ever experience such things, then they will always believe.

"If you have never experienced anything like this, then you will spend your life not believing and that is okay, I respect your beliefs. But I have had far too many things happen to me; things that there are no explanations for and I have seen and felt too many things for anyone to tell me that there is no such thing as forerunners, ghosts, spirits, etc."

She knows they do exist, she insists.

I am prepared to meet my Maker. Whether my Maker is prepared for the great ordeal of meeting me is another matter.

— Winston Churchill

Violet's Vision

In simple terms, a premonition is a foretelling of the future and as such, these visions are often considered to be a forerunner. Many people experience premonitions in everyday life, although skeptics say premonitions can be attributed to mere coincidence.

You may have experienced them. The phone rings and you know who is calling, although the call was unexpected; you have a feeling that a specific song is going to play on the radio, and it does; you think of someone you haven't seen or heard from in a while, and they suddenly show up at your home for an unannounced visit or maybe they call you out of the blue.

Premonitions are often very specific. You have a nagging,

undying feeling that something terrible is going to happen, and to one degree or another, it does. For instance, a great, unexplained feeling of sadness has been bothering you all day. You later learn that a close relative or friend has died.

There are times, however, when a premonition is so strong that there is little doubt that the events as told in the vision are going to happen. These powerful premonitions are much more rare, but happen often enough that many researchers believe they are real. Research has shown these feelings are most powerful between close relatives, where the psychic bond appears the strongest.

Premonitions can be as subtle as a gnawing feeling or they can be so overwhelming that they jolt you out of your everyday routine and prevent you from thinking of little else. They can be vague, nothing more than a feeling, or they can be so vivid that some people say it is like watching a film.

Premonitions can foretell something that happens a minute, weeks or even many months later. They can come while you're doing something as mundane as washing the dishes, or they can come in our dreams.

Regardless, they often leave you with a void or empty feeling that something tragic is about to happen.

A close bond

Violet Murphy, from the picturesque island of Cape Breton, knows all too well what it means to see into the future. She's experienced it for herself. As the second oldest of six children, she grew up keeping a close watch over her three younger brothers and younger sister.

And as the six Murphy children grew into adults and began pursuing their own lives, Violet still kept close tabs on the clan, celebrating their successes and sharing their sadness. She was the glue that kept the family together.

Cameron, the youngest Murphy child, held a special place in Violet's heart. He was an excellent student in school and an outstanding athlete, and Violet and the other members of the Murphy family beamed with pride in 1989 when their baby brother went off to university, the only one in their immediate family to do so. He was destined for greatness, they believed. They all knew Cameron could achieve anything he wanted.

Leaving home is never easy for a young person, but Cameron was determined to make the most of his opportunity. Heading off to university in Ontario with plans to first pursue a degree in business and then to study law and become a criminal lawyer, Cameron understood that he was leaving behind a family that loved him dearly.

He also knew that if for some reason things didn't work out for him in Ontario, he could always come home and he would be welcomed with open arms, no questions asked. There would be no words of disappointment, only praise and encouragement for him to follow his own life path. But Cameron worked hard, and he was a success in university.

It was during Cameron's second year in Ontario that Violet began experiencing deep feelings of sadness and sorrow that she could not explain. She felt them for several months starting in September. It was like something inside was warning her that a tragedy was about to befall the family.

A little voice

One night in December 1990, Violet's worst nightmares became reality.

Violet remembers that it was a bitterly cold night. The family was busy preparing for the holidays, and everyone was anxious for Cameron's return. They hadn't seen him since late August when he drove to Ontario to start a new semester.

Even in the midst of all the excitement, Violet could not shake a deep feeling of dread that something was not right.

On December 12, she went to bed around 10 o'clock. Her three daughters were sleeping, and her husband, Richard, was working late, so she seized the opportunity to catch up on her rest.

Richard, who had arrived home around 11 o'clock and, hoping not to disturb his sleeping wife, had gone straight to bed, jumped quickly to his feet, thinking she was ill. Violet was distraught, sobbing uncontrollably. She was shaking with such force that the entire bed was vibrating. She was nearly hysterical, trembling from head to toe.

Through her tears, she told her disbelieving husband about her dream, but she insisted that she knew it was more than a dream. She told Richard she knew it was a premonition and that Cameron was not going to make it home for Christmas.

Trying to reassure Violet that she had just had a nightmare, her husband offered to fix her some tea.

Insisting that it was more than a dream, Violet told her husband that what she had seen was more like a vision into the future. In her vision, it was evening and very dark, she told him. It had been snowing, so the roads were slippery. Cameron had been on his way back from class when he lost control of his car, skidded across the yellow line and hit an approaching truck head-on. He was killed instantly.

"He didn't have a chance," Violet sobbed. "He didn't even know what hit him."

Contrary to reassurances from Richard that her baby brother was alive and well, and despite the late hour, Violet went straight to the phone and called Cameron. Finally, after six or seven rings, the groggy, young Murphy sibling picked up the phone.

"Hello, Violet," he answered, knowing that only his older sister would phone at that time of night.

Stay off the roads

Thankful that her brother was okay, Violet told him about her premonition. She knew that he would think she was crazy, but she made him promise that he would stay off the roads after supper the following night.

Wanting to get his emotionally distraught sister off the phone so he could go back to sleep, Cameron told her that he would try. He reassured her that he would take the bus. Then, after he told her how much he loved her, he hung up and went back to sleep.

But Violet didn't sleep anymore that night. Throughout the next day and into the ensuing evening, she was restless. She tried to reach Cameron many times by phone, but had no luck. By 11 o'clock, she knew something was terribly wrong. Her brother should have been home by now. She should be able to reach him.

Just before midnight, the phone rang and her husband answered. Violet became hysterical. The call lasted no more than a minute.

Hanging up the phone, her husband quietly confirmed her worst nightmare. The call had been from the Ontario Provincial Police Department. There had been a terrible car crash, and Cameron had been killed. They believe he died instantly when the car he was driving hit an approaching truck.

I do not fear death. I had been dead for billions and billions of years before I was born, and had not suffered the slightest inconvenience from it.

— Mark Twain

When Your Dreams Come True

While folklore suggests that forerunners are usually precursors of the impending death of an individual, there are rare occurrences where such phenomena can be connected to larger events. Daisy Keyes, 81, of Chester, Nova Scotia, is one of those people who has experienced such visions.

She remembers that she was seven years old when she saw her first forerunner.

"I was sleeping in the bed with my mother who had stayed with me that night because I told her I was scared for some reason. When I woke up, I saw a large, black dog jump over the foot of the bed. Several days later a close family member died."

The family didn't have a dog but Daisy's mother explained to her that such visions are often a sign of impending death.

"I was only a child," she says. "I wasn't ready to hear talk about death and other tragedy. It was hard for me to understand it back then."

But it wasn't only forerunners she had to face, Daisy says, explaining that throughout her lifetime she had several visions of larger tragedies, not just those connected to the deaths of family members and friends.

Catastrophic wave

One of the worse visions she ever experienced occurred on Christmas night 2004 when she says she was awakened by a dream in which she saw a large wave washing over the land and killing hundreds of people. Although she had no idea where the catastrophe was going to happen, she says it was so real that she woke with a start and could immediately sense death and despair that was about to hit somewhere.

It was a very emotional experience for her, she says.

"It may have all been in my dream, but I knew when I woke up that something bad was about to happen," Daisy says, pointing out that the next day, on Boxing Day, an earth quake in the Indian Ocean created a tsunami that lead to a massive loss of life and widespread destruction. It was one of the deadliest disasters in modern history. Nearly 230,000 people died, and millions lost everything in that tragedy.

"My chest was just so heavy, it felt like I had a huge weight on me," she recalls. "I had a hard job to breathe and I just felt this great sense of loss and sadness. It was unlike I had ever experienced before."

But, she quickly adds, it wasn't the last time she experienced the sense of tremendous loss during the Christmas holidays. In 2019, Daisy says it was a particularly restless night.

"I just couldn't get to sleep," Daisy says. When she did open her eyes she saw the image of a woman appear beside her bed.

"It was a beautiful Chinese woman," Daisy says. "I remember that she was wearing a plain, straight dress along with a dusty-rose coloured blouse and a hat." This woman was looking to the west and didn't turn or look at me. The woman stayed at her bedside 15 minutes before she suddenly vanished.

Another message

The sudden appearance of this strange woman continued to haunt Daisy throughout the days that followed, but she was unable to come up with an explanation as to who she was or why she may have seen her.

"It really bothered me," she says. "Because of my experiences with this type of thing, I just knew this woman's appearance meant something."

A few days letter, Daisy says another unusual occurrence gave her an additional clue about what this woman was trying to tell her.

"A couple of nights later, I was startled out of my sleep by a bad dream," she recalls. "I had a dream about bats. There were lots of them everywhere and it really frightened me."

By the end of 2019 news reports began confirming that a new and serious respiratory illness was emerging in China and that one of the suspected origins of the highly contagious virus may have been bats. That is when Daisy put it all together.

"I believe my vision of the beautiful Chinese woman and my dream about the bats were connected and they were a warning tell me about the arrival of COVID-19," Daisy says.

Were the woman and the dream of bats a precursor of the approaching pandemic that would literally shut down the world by March 2020? Daisy says that based on her previous experiences with such phenomena she is absolutely convinced that yes, these events were, indeed, connected.

"I have had too many experiences throughout my lifetime to not believe that it was all a warning," she insists and if so, then why her? "I can't explain why these things happen to me — I just know they do."

But throughout all these "unusual" experiences she has had over the years, Daisy says she never considered the visions to be a burden.

"I never hid from it," she says, adding that sometimes she couldn't always explain the meaning right away but eventually, the truth reveals itself.

Nor was she afraid of it, she insists.

"Sometimes it left me feeling emotionally drained, but never really afraid," she says, reflecting back over her lifetime of experiences. "Truthfully," she adds, "I always considered it be a gift."

Dying is a wild night and
a new road.

— Emily Dickinson

The Christmas Bell

We have discussed forerunners throughout this book, but what about miracles? Do they exist? Are they real? Do they happen?

At least one Halifax woman insists miracles are real because she experienced one more than 55 years ago. Mary begins her story with the fact that she was only a young woman when she got married.

"It was 57 years ago and it was a different time then," she says. "Half a century ago, it was expected that women would marry young, settle down and start a family and I guess I fit right into that mold. I was okay with that. Coming from a family of nine siblings, I loved children and couldn't wait to be a mother myself. I felt it was what I was meant to do."

Mary met Lewis Bishop in 1962 when she was 18 years old and working as a sales clerk in a large retail store in Halifax; he worked on the trucks that delivered the store's stock.

Love at first sight

If love at first sight is a real thing, then Mary admits that's exactly what it was when she met Lewis.

"He was a wonderful man," she says. "He was kind and courteous, understanding and gentle. I'm not sure if I ever saw him lose his temper."

And of course, she smiles, he was very handsome, not in that Hollywood kind of way but in that natural, outdoorsman kind of way.

"Thinking back on it," Mary says, "I'm not even really sure how it all happened. It was like one day I saw him in the stockroom and the next thing I knew I was walking down the aisle, and Lewis was standing at the alter waiting for me. He was beaming from ear to ear. Come to think of it, I guess I probably was too."

While the timeframe may seem relatively short in Mary's mind, in truth the two courted for a full year. Over that time, they shared many joyous experiences that confirmed that Lewis was the man she was destined to spend the rest of her life with.

And then fate intervened.

Life, it seems, had other things in mind for Mary and Lewis.

Happy times

Just a little over a year from the day they met in June 1960, Mary and Lewis were wed in July 1961.

"It was such a beautiful day," Mary recalls, smiling warmly as she brushes a tear from her eyes. "The weather was fabulous and all our friends and family were there to celebrate with us. Lewis and I were so happy. The day was everything that a young woman would want in her wedding day."

The year 1961 was a time of major change for Lewis and Mary Bishop. Not only did they get married but Lewis took a new job with a long-haul trucking company and Mary got a promotion at the department store.

"I loved my new job and while Lewis liked his new job as well, he didn't like the fact that it took him away from home for such long periods of time," he says. "But we made the most of it because the money he earned doing that job was much better than what he had been earning driving and unloading the stock trucks at the store."

Mary says their happiness wasn't motivated by money, but they had agreed that early on in their marriage they would endure such sacrifices to make more money. They planned to save enough to purchase a home in five years and then they would start having children. At that time, Mary would quit her job so she could stay home and take care of the babies.

For the first few months of their marriage in 1961, everything was going according to that plan and they were preparing for their first Christmas together.

"We had moved into a small, one-bedroom apartment with a tiny kitchen and living room combination and a bathroom," she recalls. "It was tight, there's no doubt about that, but it was all we needed. After all, it was just Lewis and I, and I was there alone most of the time as he was on the road a lot. Furthermore, the rental price was really cheap, which meant we could add more to our savings. Besides, we were simple people; we didn't need a grand apartment."

No matter the size of the apartment, Mary says the real key was to take what she had to work with and turn it into their home. "It was comfortable and cozy and gave us everything we could ever need."

Shattered happiness

The happiness they felt together was shattered on Christmas Eve 1961 as a major blizzard hit the region hard.

"Lewis had been away for four days making a quick run to Montreal and was due back later in the afternoon of December 24," Mary recalls. "I remember that even though I was terribly worried about him being on the road in such a terrible storm, I tried to block out everything and went about with the holiday preparations. I wanted our first Christmas together as a married couple to be as perfect as I could make it, right down to the decorations and the food."

When Mary finished work at three o'clock that afternoon, she went straight home and got busy. She had lots to do, including roasting the turkey, preparing the vegetables and making the pies. Lewis loved coconut cream pie and she wanted to surprise him with a nice big one for dessert when he got home that evening.

As the snowstorm intensified on the outside, Mary kept busy

inside, trying hard not to worry about her husband, who she knew by that time was on the road somewhere between Moncton and Halifax.

"I was standing over the stove making the filling for the coconut cream pie when I suddenly got this overwhelming sense of sadness and my chest became heavy like I was having a hard time breathing. I had never felt anything like that before and I had no idea what was going on, but I knew something was wrong. I could feel it and I wanted to cry."

Still, Mary pushed on with her chores, mindful that her husband was running painfully late and trying hard to fight the growing sense of foreboding that was fluttering in the pit of her stomach.

Then she was stopped in her tracks by the sound of a bell ringing. Odd, she thought, wondering where the sound may have come from. The television and radio were both turned off.

Shrugging off the sound as nothing more than her imagination, Mary went back to work on her pie filling. Then she heard the bell again. This time she felt compelled to investigate. She went to the living room where she was sure she had heard the bell, and it rang again.

The sound was very distinct.

This time, Mary insists she heard the bell come from the Christmas tree that she and Lewis had decorated during the previous weekend before he left for Montreal.

"I heard it," she recalls. "Just as plain as day and just as clearly as I'm talking to you today."

A man's love

Approaching the tree, Mary says she immediately gazed upon the tree ornament that Lewis had bought for her to celebrate their first Christmas together. A beautiful crystal bell hung near the top of the tree as a reminder of his love for her.

"When he gave it to me on the night we decorated the tree, he promised me that he would buy me a new ornament for the tree for every Christmas that we spent together," Mary says.

Removing the bell from the Christmas tree and sitting in an old armchair that her parents had given them when they moved into the apartment, Mary says she knew something had happened to Lewis.

"I didn't know what it was but I knew it was bad," she says, her voice trembling with emotion.

After that, everything became a bit of a blur to her.

Shortly after hearing the bell ring, she heard a knock at the apartment door and when she answered it she was surprised to see her father and mother were there. Why had they ventured out in such a terrible storm, she asked them?

As it turned out, her parents were there because the police had contacted them and told them there had been a terrible accident. They told Mary that the police had contacted her father because he was a retired police officer and they felt it would be better if her parents were ones to come and tell her that Lewis's truck had been in a collision with a car instead of having a stranger show up at her door.

She learned from her parents that Lewis had swerved and took his truck over a rather steep embankment in order to avoid serious injuries to the occupants of the car. He died at the scene.

Mary was devastated, her world turned upside. In an instant, her dreams were shattered and the man she so desperately loved would never be coming home to her. She had no idea how she would go on without him.

They say time heals all wounds — even deep ones created by the tragic loss of a loved one. And in time, Mary pulled herself together and had a good life, complete with another deep love, a second marriage and children.

However, she always had a special place in her heart for Lewis, and their daughter, Louise.

You see, although Lewis died before Mary could tell him, Mary was pregnant with their daughter. She feels that somehow, deep down he knew they were going to be parents.

"I just feel that Lewis was with me that Christmas Eve and that he reached out to me through that Christmas bell as a way to let me know he was okay. I am sure of that."

And today, almost 60 years later, that bell has a special place on her Christmas tree. In time, Mary says she will give the bell to their daughter Louise as a memory of her father.

To die will be an awfully big
adventure.

— J.M. Barrie

Family Ties

When it comes to the world of the paranormal, Leigh Gibson of Kentville, Nova Scotia, believes there are different levels of awareness.

"It's not something you easily forget," Leigh says, pointing out that her first experience in the extended universe happened in 1981 when she was 11 years old. However, the events left such an indelible impression that they have remained with her throughout her entire life.

Leigh was two and a half years old the last time she saw her maternal grandfather in person so she has very few physical memories of him. Even though her family relocated to Nova

Scotia as her parents pursued employment opportunities here, she explains they maintained very close contact with family back in Missouri.

"Even though we couldn't see them, we kept in touch by phone and I regularly spoke to my grandfather whenever he and my mother talked," she says. "My mother and her father were close so they also exchanged a lot of letters. The fun part was that every time he sent a letter to mom, he also sent me personal letters of my own so I felt very close to him."

It was that strong family connection that Leigh believes led to her first experience with the paranormal.

"I remember one night when I was 11 I woke up very early from a very bad dream," she says. "It wasn't scary, but it was one of those dreams that was very disturbing, the kind that keeps you awake. I remember my mom was still up and I got up and talked to her about what I had seen."

In the dream Leigh found herself in the room of an older home that she describes as an older style sitting room or parlour and in the middle of that room there was a coffin. In the coffin was the body of a man dressed in a dark suit and tie. She could remember vivid details of the room and body, but she could not see the face of the deceased man.

"As I described the room to my mother, she told me that she immediately recognized the place," Leigh says. "She told me that I had just described the sitting room in the house in which she had grown up. I had never seen it but the family had that home for several generations."

When it came to the man in the coffin her mother had no idea who that could have been, Leigh says, but the dream left her so shaken that there was no way she was going to back to bed and falling to sleep that night. Instead, Leigh and her mother shared an early morning snack of English muffins and homemade blackberry jam.

Dream mystery solved

"Just as we finished eating, the phone rang," Leigh remembers. "It was my mother's stepmother calling to tell my mother that her father had just died."

For Leigh, it became clear in that instant that the body of the man in the coffin she had dreamed of was that of her now deceased grandfather. And while these events were very upsetting to her, she quickly adds, that they were also confirmation that she had a special connection to the paranormal world.

"I know that a lot of people don't believe in such things, but after that night I knew that I was sensitive to them," she says. "It was clear that my dream was a warning that my grandfather was going to die but at the time I just didn't know how to interpret the signs."

Second time

The second time Leigh had a paranormal experience, it was one shared with two of her sisters and it happened when she was 16 years old. The experience revolved around her father who was working at the Bedford Institute of Oceanography.

"One of my sisters was working at a Christmas tree lot and the other was living in Halifax when things began to happen that day," she says, remembering that she was attending a Sea Cadet training in camp in Lunenburg at the time.

The incident began with all three of the young women

simultaneously sharing a very distinct smell and Leigh says she recognized the odour right away.

"It was the very strong smell of my father's pipe tobacco," she says. "It was a very special blend from Virginia that had a very distinct smell of chocolate and vanilla. Our father had it sent to him and I immediately knew that's what it was. My sisters later told me they recognized it too."

Tracing the timeline of events back to the shared smell, Leigh says they discovered that about 45 minutes after that experience, her sister who worked in the Christmas tree yard was approached by the manager of the lot who told her she had to phone her mother right away because there was a family emergency.

Leigh's father had suffered from some kind of medical crisis at work and had to be rushed to the hospital.

By the time Leigh arrived at the hospital, all of her family — including her sisters and brother — were there. "That's when I found out that my father was in the operating room as he had to have emergency surgery."

After her father recovered from surgery, Leigh says she began to review the events of that day. She believes her father thought he may be going to die and reached out to his daughters in his time of need.

"I know what I smelled that day and my sisters say the same thing," she says. "We are certain that our father reached out to us when it appeared he was in trouble. We were just thankful that he didn't die that day."

And Leigh adds just because her father didn't die doesn't lessen the impact of the premonition she and her sisters shared..

People fear death even more than pain. It's strange that they fear death. Life hurts a lot more than death. At the point of death, the pain is over. Yeah, I guess it is a friend.

— Jim Morrison

A Mother's Intuition

Call it a gut feeling. Call it a sixth sense. Call it intuition. Haven't you — hasn't everybody — ever known something with certainty even though you can't explain how you know it?

It is possible that all of us have the gift of intuition, but only a few are able to tap into it. Mothers, though, are highly intuitive, especially when it comes to the wellbeing of their children.

There have been many documented cases of mothers intuitively knowing when their children were in trouble, even when great distances have separated them. Many a time a mother has felt a strong urge to reach out to her child and followed that instinct only to find her child was in distress.

Helen and her husband Arthur, who spoke on the condition that they could remain anonymous, had three children, all boys. Arthur was a fisherman who had toiled on the North Atlantic his entire life and while he earned a good, honest living from the sea, he would be the first to agree that it was also a hard life. The days were long and the conditions were dangerous. Arthur survived many close calls during his lifetime.

Working on the sea was all Arthur knew and like his own father and all the men from his family who came before him, he was content with the life he had created for his family. Be that as it may, it wasn't a life that he wanted for any of his boys. He hoped his children would grow up and find jobs that would provide a good lifestyle for their own families but as fate would have it, all three of Arthur's sons followed him to sea and all three were happy and content to do so.

Helen worried about her sons. She had spent her entire married life worrying and fretting over the safety of her husband and as each of her sons grew up and took to the open sea she took on the burden of worry for each of them as well.

Life on the high seas

It was a heavy load to carry on her shoulders. She knew first-hand the perils of the life of a fisherman as she had lost many members of her own family to tragedies on the ocean, including her older brother.

She waited with baited breath each and every time Arthur or any of her sons went to work. It was not easy to remain ashore not knowing what her loved ones were facing so many miles out on the open seas. She coped and prayed, accepting that such was the life of a fisherman's wife and mother.

Helen had a deep bond with all three of her sons, but that bond ran deepest with her youngest son, Jimmy. Perhaps it was that bond or her intuition that led her to know something was wrong in 1996.

As her two oldest sons grew up, married, and then moved out of the house to start their own families, Jimmy remained behind. That arrangement was just fine with Helen. She knew the day would come when her son would meet someone and move out, but she was prepared to pepper her youngest child with as much love and affection as she could while he was still at home.

She liked having her son around the house, but she loathed those times when he went to sea for she feared he might not return. Sometimes, as the job demanded, Jimmy would be gone for four or five days at a time and those long trips were especially hard on his mother.

When he wasn't fishing, Jimmy liked to party, sometimes not returning home until late into the night. This, of course, caused Mom to worry and she spent many a sleepless night wondering what her youngest son was up to and if he was okay.

Rules are rules

Helen didn't sleep much when Jimmy was out with his friends and because he was still living under her roof, she had one rule that she insisted he follow. She didn't ask any questions because her son was an adult, but no matter what time he came in at night, she insisted that he come to tell her that he was home and that everything was okay.

Knowing how much this meant to his mother, Jimmy followed the rule without protest and whenever he came home, no matter the time, he would go directly to his parents' bedroom, stand in the doorway, and announce that he was okay. With that reassurance from her son, Helen was then able to fall asleep.

Sometimes the hour was very late and while he hated to bother them, he also knew his mother would not be sleeping and would be waiting to hear from him. While the routine was borne from the elderly woman's worries about her son's wellbeing, in time, it became a running joke between the two but the practice continued for many years.

Shortly after Jimmy's 26th birthday, he was preparing for a fishing trip that his captain estimated would last four or five days. Including the captain, there were four crewmembers on board and Jimmy brought home a good payday for his long hours of work.

He was looking forward to this trip because he was saving money for a down payment on a house that he had been eyeing and he estimated that these earnings would give him enough to finally make the purchase.

However, in the days leading up to her son's departure, Helen couldn't shake the feeling that something was terribly wrong. She couldn't quite explain it, but she felt there was a dark cloud hanging over her family and she feared something terrible was about to happen.

As her husband had retired and neither of her older sons were scheduled to go out in the near future, she couldn't shake the feeling that whatever was about to happen must involve Jimmy.

Fearing the worst, she tried for days to convince Jimmy to skip this trip, telling him that he didn't need the money and offering to pay whatever difference he needed for his down payment on the house.

But Jimmy wasn't having any of that and on the morning of his departure Jimmy kissed his mother goodbye as he always did, and told her he would see her in four or maybe five days. As he left through the kitchen, he paused at the back door and turned back to tell her not to worry.

Something was wrong

But Helen was not so sure about that and as she watched her youngest son walk down the back steps and disappear down the back walkway on his way to the wharf, she felt a deep gnawing in the pit of her stomach. Something was wrong, she believed, fearing she would never see her son again.

As the next two days crept by, the dark cloud followed Helen wherever she went. She could not shake the oppressive feeling that tragedy was near. She prayed that her son and his fellow crewmembers were okay and that they would make it safely back to port.

On the night of the second day of Jimmy's trip, Helen was having an especially difficult time sleeping. Tossing and turning, she remembers glancing at the digital clock on the night table next to her bed. In glowing red numbers, the clock said it was 12:15 a.m.

Just then, she felt a strong urge to turn around and when she did, she was surprised to see Jimmy standing in the doorway. He said to her, "Don't worry, Mom. Everything is okay. You can go to sleep now."

While Helen was surprised to see Jimmy standing there, because he wasn't due back in port for at least another two days, perhaps even three, as a fisherman's wife she also knew that many things can happen out at sea that may force the boat to return earlier than scheduled.

Perhaps there was engine trouble. Perhaps the catch was good and they filled their hold early. Perhaps someone was sick or injured and needed medical attention. Perhaps there was a storm at sea that they didn't know about back on land. Whatever was going on, Helen took comfort in knowing that Jimmy was home and knowing that she could get the details from him in the morning, she rolled over and went to sleep.

The next morning as Helen and Arthur were in the kitchen having breakfast the telephone rang. She quickly picked up the receiver after the first ring because she didn't want the noise to wake her son.

As Helen spoke to whoever was on the phone, Arthur could tell something was wrong as he watched his wife turn every shade of white he could imagine. Quickly placing her hand over the phone, she told him to go upstairs and check on Jimmy.

Without questioning his wife's instructions, Arthur immediately went up the stairs. When he returned a few minutes later, he told his wife that Jimmy was not in his bed and that it did not look like the bed had been slept at all.

"No," Helen cried, dropping the phone. She insisted that Jimmy had come home last night and that he had spoken to her.

Picking up the phone, Arthur listened while one of captains from the wharf told him that Jimmy's boat was missing and that they had no contact with them since 12:15 a.m.

According to the man from the wharf, that was the last time that any known transmission was sent from Jimmy's boat and it was feared that the boat and all four crewmembers had been lost.

But how could that be? That's a question that haunted Helen in the years following the tragedy.

"I knew something was wrong," she said. "I knew Jimmy was in trouble long before that boat went down."

Had Helen seen Jimmy's forerunner, a celestial image of a person in distress or imminent danger? Did the young man reach out to his mother during the last few minutes of his life to let her know he was okay?

Helen went to her grave thinking yes he did.

I want to go on living after my death!
And that's why I'm so grateful to
God for having given me this gift,
which I can use to develop myself and
to express all that's inside me!

— Anne Frank

Epilogue

Are forerunners real or are they nothing more than the result of an overactive imagination?

Do overly engaged emotions lead to a manifestation of these experiences or are forerunners a merging of our world with the paranormal?

Is that paranormal plane real?

Why do some people experience forerunners and others do not?

Are some people more in touch with the paranormal world than others?

Why do common, everyday superstitions mostly dwell on death, but few remind us of the more positive occurrences in our lives?

These are all very good questions but as with all things paranormal there are no simple answers and no hard-fast rules as to what is fact and what is imagined. And sadly, there is no hard and fast physical evidence to support the argument that any paranormal presence exists except eye witness accounts.

The bottom line is this — what you accept as fact and what you choose to believe are your decisions to make.

In the preceding pages, we've presented first-hand accounts of individuals who experienced these phenomena. While their stories are compelling, they may also seem farfetched or to too fantastical to be true. So, you, dear reader, will have to decide whether or not you believe them.

I choose to believe.

—Vernon Oickle

We die. That may be the meaning of life. But we do language. That may be the measure of our lives.

— Toni Morrison

Omens of death

According to Maritime superstition …

- It is a sign of impending death if a window in your home suddenly slams shut on its own.
- It is a sign of impending death if a mirror suddenly cracks or falls from the wall and smashes.
- It is a sign of impending death if an empty pot falls to the floor. If the pot is full and falls to the floor, then it means someone close to you is going to die.
- It is a sign of impending death if you hear someone whisper your name in your ear.
- It is a sign of impending death if you hear three distinct knocks on a door (or wall) and there is no one there.
- It is a sign of impending death of someone you know if a bird hits your window. If a bird gets into your house, then it's a sign that someone in your family is going to die.
- It is a sign of impending death if you hear a bell tolling in the distance which no one else can hear.
- It is a sign of impending death if a picture or a calendar falls from the wall for no apparent reason.
- It is a sign of impending death if you see a vision of someone close to you who really isn't there.
- It is a sign of impending death if you hear a dog howling outside a house at night but you don't have a dog.
- It is a sign of impending death if plants and trees bloom out of season.

- It is a sign of impending death if you hear an owl hooting during the day or if you see an owl perched on your house.
- It is a sign of impending death if you hear a cricket singing in the house.
- It is a sign of impending death if a mouse is discovered in the house.
- It is a sign of impending death on the farm if a calf was stillborn or if the hens nest in the morning.
- It is a sign of impending death if you dream of a white horse.
- It is a sign of impending death if you see a single crow in a cemetery.
- It is a sign of impending death if you dream of the dead.
- It is a sign of impending death if a crow sits on your clothesline.
- It is a sign of impending death if you place a hat on a bed.
- It is a sign of impending death if a clock that has not been working suddenly chimes.
- It is a sign of impending death if you see three seagulls flying in a row.
- It is a sign of impending death if you dream you are falling.
- It is a sign of impending death if you dream of white flowers.
- It is a sign of impending death if you ring a bell unnecessarily on board a ship because it means a sailor somewhere is going to die.